PERSPECTIVES

⬥➤ FROM THE ⬥➤

CHOIR LOFT

MARK WILKEN

WESTBOW
P R E S S®
A DIVISION OF THOMAS NELSON
& ZONDERVAN

WestBow Press books may be ordered through booksellers or by contacting:

WestBow Press
A Division of Thomas Nelson & Zondervan
1663 Liberty Drive
Bloomington, IN 47403
www.westbowpress.com
844-714-3454

Cover Photograph, "Chapel Organ Loft at Valparaiso University," by Edward Byrne
Used by permission. All rights reserved worldwide.

Scripture taken from the King James Version of the Bible.

ISBN: 978-1-6642-2581-7 (sc)
ISBN: 978-1-6642-2582-4 (hc)
ISBN: 978-1-6642-2580-0 (e)

Library of Congress Control Number: 2021904375

Print information available on the last page.

WestBow Press rev. date: 03/26/2021

CONTENTS

PREFACE

I t's a new day, the day after yesterday. During this day, anything can happen. The possibilities for today are essentially limitless, either for the better or the worse. It's not so much that you control this day; rather you are a part of it, and it is about to be a part of you. It's not appropriate to think that you control the workings of today, for that is left only to God, the one who created you—the one who understands not only who you are, but what you are and what you are capable of. The issue then is this: If God is, in fact, who He says He is, then you have a variety of important truths you need to confront—not only today, but every day of your life.

You see, you are fearfully and wonderfully made. You were no accident. You are not a random occurrence. Rather you are a gem! You are something beautiful to behold. You are the result of the incredible perfect creative genius of God. But to quote one of my best friends, "Don't get the big head." Everything you have read to this point was brought about not by your own direct intervention or any input initiated by you. It was caused as part of God's perfect plan, devised, orchestrated, and controlled by Him.

In Genesis 1, beginning at verse 26, God decides to create men and women in His image. Now it is far too easy to brush past this simple phrase without fully considering its potential implications, not only for you but every person you will ever meet. However, it's not only that God created you in His image, but that He knew you intimately long before you were born. Psalm 139 describes the intimacy that exists between human beings and our Creator. Never before or since has our relationship with God been casual or indifferent. He knows you equally intimately now. Additionally, you are not just some random thing or being that He assembled and flippantly threw into the mix to see how things might play out. God, our Father, put the entire package of who and what you are together for a well-defined reason at this moment in time. You are not here as part of some computer simulation or hypothetical game concocted by God for His sole personal amusement. You were given life because God considered enjoying a relationship with you as something vital and worthy of pursuit.

I grew up attending church with my family. During my junior high years, I turned my life over to the Lord and accepted Christ as my personal Savior. I've walked with the Lord for many years; although, it's probably more accurate to say that He's walked beside me for each of the sixty years I've lived on this planet, I think it's also fair to say that He's spent a good bit of His precious time trying to get me to become the person He knows I can be. The person He designed me to be. Although I've come a good long distance down the road with Christ, I believe I still have much to learn. Just as importantly, I believe the experiences I'm having here are preparing me for something even greater going forward. I can't tell you what the future holds for me or anyone else. What I can tell you is that the one who holds the future is holding on to me.

PURPOSE

The following pages represent a collection of devotional ideas that I hope will stir your heart. I believe some of them might make you laugh, while others may tug at your heartstrings. Ultimately I hope that these articles will prompt you to take a candid look at the message of truth contained in scripture and allow it to deeply move your heart. One more important point must be made now. The Bible is both authoritative and worthy of consideration for direction as to how to live your life. The words I have written in the following pages are merely intended to highlight the truths contained in scripture. No mere human being, regardless of their position in life, can presume to usurp the authority of scripture by anything they say, write, or believe.

Given the above, I invite you to delve into God's word, the Bible, and learn it, study it, and take it to heart. The Bible is foundational and true. Nothing else compares. Nothing else is worth it.

Finally, just because someone will probably ask, yes, I have been a choir member for many years. Interestingly, I think it has given me a slightly different perspective on how people perceive the Bible and its relevance to their lives. I hope my thoughts will bless you.

MARK WILKEN

WHAT DO YOU DO WHEN WHAT YOU DO IS NOT GOOD ENOUGH?

PSALM 112

We all have involvements. Some are very significant, impacting our communities and changing lives and ideas. Others are less lofty, focused on individuals and their personal dreams and aspirations. Regardless of the focus, our involvements reflect much about who and what we are. These involvements and interests give life meaning and value. Remove them, and you remove a reason to exist, a foundation stone of your life.

All of us desire, at least at some level, to impact the world, to make a difference. We want our lives to mean something, if not to others, then at least to ourselves. In the final analysis, it really is the value others place upon us that truly supports our self-concept. We may be fairly independent in our perception of ourselves, but if we cannot externally verify that our perception is rational, we have no proof of the validity of our opinion. In other words, it takes multiple independent observations to verify a fact, even if that fact is as simple as our own self-esteem.

So what happens when you put your best foot forward and things turn out poorly? What happens when your best intentions result in others' scorn? Your goal may have been honorable and noteworthy, but instead of garnering favor, you inspire ill will. In short, what do you do when you fail? Worse yet, what do you do when you succeed, but your success falls short of others' perception of excellence?

None of us are perfect. There is nothing we can achieve in this life potentially elevating us to the level of perfection perceived universally as such. We are imperfect creatures living in an imperfect world. Our efforts will always be limited by our own shortcomings and limited intellect. That doesn't mean, however, that our activities and interests are without honor or merit. It's not that we can't achieve anything great; it's more about how our achievements will be considered by those whom we respect the most.

There is no shortage of opportunity in the world. Everywhere we look, everywhere we go, situations exist for us to make a difference. The question is: will we recognize them when they present themselves? Additionally, if we're inclined to do something, will our actions bring about positive, if not excellent, results? Finally, what if we try to make a difference but fail?

The simple fact is that we don't always succeed. That our best may not be good enough is not sufficient reason not to try. Importantly, we must remember God put us here for a reason. His definition of success is different than our own. Accordingly, something we deem a failure may be a resounding success in His eyes. An important key to remember is that finishing the race is often more important than winning. Finishing well is more important than winning with a smug attitude. It's better to spend a day with someone humble about their endeavors than with someone who constantly reminds you of their successes.

Remember, God knows what you do. He appreciates your best efforts, even when the results come up short. So we must learn to measure our character, successes, or failures on God's scale, a scale calibrated more to His glory rather than the results we achieve.

TAKE ME TO THE DEEP END

PROVERBS 2

The diving board beckoned. Kids were jumping off, diving, and having a great time. I wasn't one of them. I couldn't swim. At six, the ability to swim had not yet been imparted to me. Life was defined by and limited to the shallow end. Most of the time that was okay, that is, until I saw the fun they were having in the deep end.

I dearly wanted to jump off the diving board. What a great time I could have. But there was a problem. I couldn't swim, an essential part of surviving in deep waters. Of course there was a solution. It made a lot of sense to me. So I presented it to my dad. "You can catch me," I told him.

The solution seemed logical to me. After all, that's what he had always done in the shallow end. He would wait for me in the water, and I would jump off the side to him. He was always there, and he always rescued me. The possibility of an adventure in the deep end looked bright.

"No!" It wasn't going to happen. What a cold, harsh reality. How could Dad be so heartless? At six, I didn't consider that Dad couldn't touch the bottom in the deep end. Catching me was more than just a simple problem. Both of our lives would be at risk. And he wasn't having it. His solution was that I had to learn how to swim on my own. Nuts! I didn't know how to swim on my own. I had spent all of my time in the shallow end, never worrying too much about my inability to swim ... until now.

After several attempts to get Dad to reconsider, it became obvious he was not moving. It's funny how parents can be like that. Finally I relented. I would learn how to swim. The diving board was still calling my name. I wasn't giving up. Dad was kind enough to give me some pointers. "Kick your feet, move your arms like this (illustrating with his own), and lay out flat in the water. And, oh yes, turn your head to breathe." It was simple. Anyone could do it!

Given my vast experience to that point, I tried to do just what he said. I paddled vigorously, barely keeping my head above the water. I maintained my ability to breathe, but little else. I got the kicking, paddling with my arms, and breathing; it was the laying down to move forward I had a hard time with. When I laid flat in the water, I tended to sink. The result: I learned to swim underwater before I learned to swim on top. So, I would dog paddle to get a breath and then swim underwater to get where I wanted to go. It was unconventional, but it worked.

Proudly, I showed my dad I was now an accomplished swimmer, fully qualified to jump off the diving board into the deep end. After a couple trips across the pool with my, shall I say, creative swimming style, he, I'm sure reluctantly, agreed to let me begin my diving career.

I was awkward, uncoordinated, and inexperienced, but I had also achieved. That day I entered a new world previously unavailable and unexplored. It was a small thing, but an important milestone. I grew because I asked. I was challenged, I was willing to try, and I learned. My solution wasn't elegant, but I gave it my best shot, and it was accepted.

We need to understand that our heavenly Father works much the same way. Because He understands the risks and is aware of our skills (or lack thereof), He limits our options so as not to set us up to fail. In other words, He will not let us jump into the deep end until He is confident we can swim. He encourages us to study and gain the understanding we need to succeed in life. He is not worried about our initial uncoordinated efforts. He's concerned that we grow in Him and become all He designed us to be. So go ahead! Dive in, but don't be surprised if God requires you to learn how to swim first.

THE RAT RACE: WHO DECIDES WHO WINS?

COLOSSIANS 3:18–4:1

W e do it every day. We get up, get ready, jump in the car, run to the office, and rejoin the rat race. We toil through our day, checking things off our to-do lists and promptly setting up new ones. The hours fold into days, the days into weeks, and the weeks into years. Some of us are blessed, and we enjoy what we do. Others aren't so fortunate. We work day in and day out, and after a while, we wonder what it's all about. We wonder why we do what we are doing.

The problem is that it's easy to get caught up in the activity in our daily lives. We tend to lose sight of the real meaning and purpose behind why we are here. I've noticed when I get particularly stressed, it becomes difficult to remember my purpose in life. I begin focusing only on managing my schedule and accomplishing the next task on the list. I become fatigued because the unaccomplished tasks greatly outnumber the completed ones, not to mention my shortage of available resources. After a while, I sometimes become overwhelmed and simply want to throw up my hands and quit.

I don't think I'm alone in this problem. I think many people out there feel the same way. They're frustrated with their jobs or, worse yet, their lives. They're into a career that has lost its appeal, if it ever had one in the first place. They're at a loss about what to do next. Each day becomes increasingly frustrating. They may suffer the oppression of a power-obsessed boss who is in love with his/her own importance, or they may simply have too many bills to consider a change of careers.

Life is not as whimsical as most of us wish it would be. We are not afraid to work hard, but we wonder if our efforts make any difference to anyone. We consider that in twenty or thirty years, we will complete a career. We wonder if any of it will matter to anyone, anywhere, anytime.

In short, we wonder if there is any purpose behind our lives. And if so, what is it?

I think it's fair to say we all want to matter. Each of us wants our life to count for something meaningful, something that will outlast our short stay on this small planet. My simple response to that is with Christ, it can, and it does. Everything we do in this life has meaning and purpose. God is aware of our every move and motive. He is involved in every situation and concerned about every element of our lives. The hard part is to remember this truth as we walk through each day with Him at our side.

Christ loves us! That is a very simple truth that's too easily overlooked or marginalized. It is the truth that will sustain you through all of life's ups and downs. In Colossians 3:18–4:1, we are reminded for whom it is that we are working. It isn't necessarily those we see, although they obviously benefit, but the one we don't see. When we work, we work for the Lord. The benefits of our toils are not temporal; rather they are eternal. We work for the Lord in all we do. When we realize this and take it to heart, our careers and occupations assume a completely different meaning. We can more easily become passionate about something when we understand it is for the Lord's benefit. Pursuing complicated or costly endeavors in terms of time and/or resources becomes compelling instead of intimidating. Persistence through the mundane transforms into an opportunity to bless someone you love. In short, life regains its joy because all you're called upon to do is now an offering, a gift for the Lord you love.

So you see, the rat race isn't about being a rat. It's about taking the blessings of God and using them for His purpose in a world crying out for the truth and love of God. That's a good thing to know when things start getting you down.

OK, I KNOW CHRIST, BUT AM I WILLING TO LET HIM KNOW ME?

PSALM 51

OK, it's honesty time. The "me" people know and see is not the me I live with. The external me is based on the image I want to have. It's a function of the traits and personality I choose to let people see. Most of what comes out is genuine and real, but it is not the whole story. Pieces are missing. I'm purposely withholding those elements because they are attributes I don't like or deem others will reject.

I do not believe I'm any different than most everyone else. That's both a relief and a frustration. It's a relief because I know everyone has their hang-ups and faults, so I'm not unique in that respect. It's frustrating because I truly want to be known and known intimately for who I really am.

Relationships are based on truth and love between people who have decided to share a part of their lives with each other. The less that is held back, the deeper the relationship can go. Unfortunately, the depth most of us share never gets us out of the shallow end of the pool. Such is the situation with most, if not all, of our human relationships. They are limited by our fears of being hurt or exposed, probably because we've been harmed in the past or we're ashamed of some of our past choices. As a result, they fall short of our hopes and dreams, and we often find our lives come up short of our expectations and desires.

Now, I'm not a cynic; neither am I a defeatist. It's just I've noticed my defensive tendencies in my relationships with other people tend to carry over into my life with Christ, which is a major concern. The one relationship in my life that should be perfect is anything but. What makes matters worse is that I know who is at fault in the situation. Obviously it's me! That smarts. No casting off blame here. No deflecting responsibility. It all rests with me. It's a situation demanding change, and the one who has to accomplish the change is me.

Now don't get me wrong. I know as a Christian, the Holy Spirit is working within my heart, prompting me to move closer to Christ every day. Philippians 1:6 points this out very succinctly. However, my faith in Christ doesn't cause my free will to evaporate. I still have to decide to continually and completely surrender my life to Christ. It's a constant process of dedication and devotion to the Lord I love. It's not a one-day process. It requires a long-term commitment of effort and energy. I know the Holy Spirit is doing His part. It's up to me to do mine.

Perhaps you feel similarly about your relationship with Christ. Perhaps things come up short in your heart as well. Well, there is hope for both of us. The bottom line is Christ loves us all, including all of our faults and hang-ups. You see, Christ approaches relationships differently than we do. He doesn't enter the fray without full knowledge of who we are, what our problems are, and what our lives are all about. We don't have to worry about keeping certain things secret because he knows everything we know, including the things we have forgotten.

Knowing and loving Christ is an opportunity to have a friend with whom you can have complete trust. He will not abandon nor condemn you. He will love you, sometimes despite yourself, and He completely accepts you even though you may have some significant faults. Trust Christ. Let Him know you. Give your life to Him, and let Him be your friend.

FAITH AND BUSINESS
DON'T MIX ... NOT!

2 KINGS 12:6–16

"It's not spiritual!" "It's not holy!" "It doesn't allow for the movement of the Spirit!" "The two should be divorced from one another!" All of these are notions about the combination of faith and business, and they're all wrong.

I first heard some of these objections when I served as the treasurer of my church. To be honest, I was shocked, not to mention disappointed. I can't think of anything that could be further from the truth. Not only is it important to carry on the activities of the church efficiently and wisely, but it's also vital to add faithfulness into our business practices.

As has been the case in recent years, there are Christians who believe business activities, not to mention politics, are worldly at best and downright evil at worst. Their belief usually stems from real-world experiences with unscrupulous businesspeople who throw ethics out the window in their relentless pursuit of a profit. Moreover, they observe some of the most successful executives falling to the temptation to steal and cheat their way to the top. Sadly, some of the most notable scoundrels also claim to be Christians. They show up at church on Sunday, politely listen to the sermon, and then return to work on Monday applying the same unethical business practices and acting as if the visit to church never happened.

Sadly, the problem is not limited to the external business world but occurs within the church itself. The difference between the two venues simply reverses the problem. In the church, people tend to leave their business acumen at the door and try to handle issues strictly based on faith. Unfortunately, the philosophy develops that says we need to reach out in faith and not worry about the business aspects of a decision. Both of these positions are flawed.

In reality, God expects us to be business-minded and act faithfully simultaneously. The two concepts should function together as a balanced unit, not as independent mutually exclusive concepts. Throughout the Bible, we have been given numerous examples of good business practices, handshaking with faithfulness. In the instances where a balance is struck, the results are positive, receiving a commendation from God. Alternatively, dishonest and faithless practices are criticized and shunned, not to mention potentially deadly as in the case of Ananias and Sapphira (Acts 5:1–11).

Consider this passage in 2 Kings. Repairs were needed for the temple. Certainly the need reflected upon the faithfulness of the people, but it also played to the practical element of the stewardship of the Lord's resources. Work needed to be done. Completion of the work would have a direct correlation with the faith of the people, but the work had to be managed. It had to be paid for, and it had to be done right.

It's the same in our churches and businesses as well. God gave us the blessing of a brain, and He expects us to use it morally and ethically. He also encourages us to act on the faith He put in our hearts. The two are neither randomly occurring nor mutually exclusive. They are two sides of the same coin. It's our job to make the connection function to further the Lord's work and expand the kingdom for His glory.

YOU MAY HAVE THE KEYS TO THE CHURCH, BUT THAT DOESN'T MEAN YOU OWN IT

MATTHEW 21:12–17

You know them. They've been there for years. They remember each of the last five pastors. They or their parents were founders of the church. One of their family members has sat on the board of elders or deacons for the majority of the last thirty years. They've seen the church through the good and bad times. They've been faithful and consistent, and everyone knows who they are.

Every church has its longtime members. They are people who understand commitment and tenacity. Enduring all of the ups and downs, they could always be counted on to support the ministry in body, if not in spirit. Usually these are wonderful people who know how to live for the Lord and have been consistent in their faith for many years. They're not afraid to stand up for the faith and have lived lives to prove it. These are not the people we're concerned with here!

Within some churches, some individuals have found their way onto boards and other positions of authority, whose motives don't particularly line up with the Great Commission. These people know how to look the part and talk the talk but have some serious control issues. These folks would like to maintain the church at the current status quo for fear of the potential changes that might occur contrary to their liking. They often quibble with the pastor about any newly proposed programs, and they routinely object to newcomers being allowed to have any position of authority. In short, they have constructed a power structure around themselves and their close associates to control the entire operation of the church. They are in charge, and they like for people to know it. They are toxic leaders who are more interested in maintaining the status quo than becoming a catalyst for growth.

The problem is that they shouldn't be in charge. Their positions of authority tend to do more to thwart the furtherance of the gospel than encourage it. Instead of welcoming new members openly, they tend to erect barriers, making people who don't fit the mold feel unwelcome. Necessary changes and improvements to the ministry are rejected out of hand, and new ideas are generally frowned upon. The thought of installing new people on any of the boards is unacceptable to this group, and they insist on overseeing every major decision.

Ultimately these people drive others from the church. The cold and restrictive environment fostered by them deflects progress on spiritual growth and outreach to our lost world. Newcomers find it easier to move on than move in, and evangelism is stifled. The body of believers stagnates under their leadership. At this point, the church is no longer a ministry; rather it becomes an empty religious organization that ultimately sinks under its own weight.

Christ fought the entrenched church leadership of his day. They too had lost the vision of God's message to the world, and their churches became empty of meaning and devoid of truth. It's our responsibility as believers to foster a church environment that is open to the changes the Holy Spirit is trying to bring about. It's also important for those of us who are in a position of authority to be mindful that Christ defined a leader as a servant of the people.

Leaders must be ever mindful of the impact that they have on the kingdom of God and its existing and future members. It is our responsibility to help the spiritual growth of others endeavoring to have an intimate relationship with Christ, including grooming them, in time, to take the reins of leadership as well. Remember, you may have the keys to the church, but they really belong to Christ. He is the Master. At most, you are merely the doorkeeper who is expected to welcome new members into the kingdom.

YOU CAN'T TRULY LEAD
UNTIL YOU'VE FAILED

MATTHEW 26:31–35; JOHN 21:15–19

Peter: what a man! He was a devout disciple who loved our Savior and dearly desired to serve Him. He showed courage when others ran and stayed near to Christ when others were nowhere to be found. Yet Peter was still human. He still faced a crisis with the limitation of his faculties and understanding of the future. Christ warned Peter that he (Peter) would deny Him when the time came, despite the honest desire of Peter's heart to do otherwise. An arrest in the garden, an attack with a sword, and an angry mob later, Peter's moment arrived. Confronted with the test, Peter denied he even knew Jesus, arguably his closest friend. He stepped back from the confrontation, and he failed. Immediately he realized everything had changed. Brokenhearted, he ran out and wept bitterly (Matthew 26:75).

It's not an unfamiliar story. Peter's actions are usually prominently featured in the annual Easter pageant, not to mention the subject of several sermons throughout the year. Usually the subject of a message on forgiveness, Peter is typically seen as the disciple who was reinstated after Christ's resurrection. Certainly this was true, but there is something more to be seen here as well.

Peter did something not foreign to many of us today. He knew the Savior and promised Him he would stand for and by Him, but when things got tough, Peter caved in. When the time came to stand by Christ, Peter swore he didn't even know Him. Any way you cut it, Peter didn't live up to the faith he claimed to profess. I could be critical of Peter, giving numerous theological reasons why what he did was atrocious, but in doing so, I would be a hypocrite.

You see, Peter did something I've done numerous times in my life. I failed my Lord. Now I'm not talking about the simple garden-variety failures, but heart-wrenching, I-can't-believe-a-Christian-would-do-that kind of failure, the kind that turns your guts inside out and makes you wonder if your salvation really took! You may have been there yourself. (If not, watch out. Every dog gets his day.) It's not a fun place to be. Once you've been there, you really try to avoid going there again.

There is also something else reassuring about Peter's story; Christ used him boldly to establish the church here on earth after His ascension. Instead of writing Peter off as an irredeemable turncoat, Christ lovingly showed His confidence in him and encouraged him to be an effective minister of the gospel.

Peter learned from Christ, and he learned from his own mistakes as well. Not only did he grow from his time with the Lord, but he also took to heart the impact of his actions that disappointed Him. I'm thankful for Peter because he gives me hope. I believe that the Lord can use me even though I am a broken vessel prone to failure. Peter served the Lord despite his shortcomings, and when future tests came, he met them victoriously. Peter was seasoned and strengthened by his failure, just as we are when we come up short in the achievement column. You don't have to be perfect to serve the Lord. In fact, the imperfections often serve to point us back in the right direction, give us strength, and convince us of Christ's forgiving love.

MAJORING ON OUR MINORS: REASONS THE BODY OF BELIEVERS IS SUFFERING FROM THE FLU

EPHESIANS 4:1–16

W hen you read this, you may take offense. You may politely disagree, you may smile and dismiss what I've said with no further thought, or you might just concur. Such is the state of affairs in the body today. We take positions on issues across the spectrum of our faith which put us in agreement with some and out of sync with others. We know the basics of our faith. We gather in congregations of people who understand the faith similarly and with whom we tend to agree on major issues. We find it easy to sing along with our favorite hymns, and we enjoy a sense of belonging. Everything works well until the day arrives when someone disagrees.

Every Sunday people meet in congregations across the world to praise the Lord and declare unity in the faith. Unfortunately, the unity is conspicuously absent among believers in the same community. Too often, we attend different churches in different denominations because the differences among us have become the focus, not the Redeemer who binds us together. We point out our differences with pride and develop long disciplinary statements to support the reasons for remaining apart. We too often find it easy to point out why what someone else believes is in error, while supporting what we believe as being closer to the heart of God.

Now don't get me wrong. I'm not suggesting that in the name of trying to get along we should adopt a watered-down faith based on some universalistic conglomeration of beliefs that omits Christ from the center of all things. I'm talking about embracing a Christ-centered, Bible-believing evangelical faith founded on the absolute reliability of scripture. Furthermore, individual believers, churches, and denominations must be well grounded in the truth that celebrates the lordship of Christ and effectively presents the gospel to those who do not know Him. Unfortunately, far too many of these individuals and organizations have simply forgotten how vital it is for them to get along. Instead of celebrating the common ground they can share in the love of Jesus Christ, they accentuate the differences they have over issues not central to the faith. They choose little hills of disagreement to die on instead of defending the big mountains of the Christian faith that all believers should stand on.

That there are differences of opinion on certain issues is not new to faith in God. Even in the days of Christ and Paul, there were differences among believers. Paul taught these churches at length about unity because he knew, at least in part, people tend to go their own way and cause divisions. Interestingly, Paul did not teach compromise. He did not teach a watered-down faith where the members had to sacrifice the truth in order to get along. On the contrary, Paul taught strict adherence to the truth, even when it was unpopular and/or the majority felt otherwise.

There is never an easy solution to dealing with honest differences of opinion regarding correct interpretation of scripture. Paul and Christ are not here to get involved in the discussion. We, however, are here, and while we haven't been given perfect knowledge and wisdom, we have been given something else. We've been given love. There will be disagreements about scripture until Christ returns, but there doesn't have to be any argument about forgiveness, mercy, unity, and love. When we learn to exercise these, we will have less separation because of our differences. Moreover, we will tend to focus less on our minors and more on our majors. Unity is found in Christ when He remains our primary focus.

YOU CAN DO ALL THINGS! BUT WILL YOU LIVE THAT LONG?

PHILIPPIANS 4:10–20

I like to ask people what they want to be when they grow up. It's an interesting question, all too often forgotten as we move further into our lives and careers. Surprisingly, very few people have given it much thought; they are focused instead upon the tasks at hand, like keeping up with the kids. Looking forward to future opportunities or even considering the possibilities is too often deemed irrelevant or too tedious a task.

Personally, my concern is not with whether or not to evaluate the possibilities; rather it is with focusing on which ones can be achieved in this lifetime. As of this writing, I have at least ten career-oriented alternatives I would like to pursue. My problem is not with developing enjoyable alternatives. It's with figuring out which opportunities to pursue and when, not to mention for how long.

God blessed each of us with talents and skills to be applied to pursuing the dreams He placed in our hearts. It is our responsibility to utilize those talents in ways that provide the greatest benefit to others and ourselves while bringing glory to God. We were designed to be productive, contributing positively to this society of which we are a part. Each day we live is an opportunity to be a blessing while enjoying our relationship with the Father.

Importantly, we need to realize each stage of our lives affords us new and intriguing opportunities impossible or impractical at other times. Too often we adopt the opinion we are too old to try something new or make a significant career move. On the other hand, we may feel we are stuck doing something until our kids are gone or because we simply can't afford a change. Nothing could be further from the truth. At almost any age, we can pursue any opportunity we choose, assuming our health and skills allow.

Do you wish to go back to school? Sign up and go! Today you can take classes from numerous colleges and universities in the comfort of your own home. Want to start your own business? A wide variety of groups and individuals wait to provide assistance and direction for virtually any endeavor you can conceive. To a great degree, your greatest hindrance is your own ability to dream.

When God put Adam and Eve in the garden of Eden, He gave them things to do that encouraged developing their creative skills. He wanted them to be fruitful and multiply. I don't believe He was strictly focused on having children. I believe He wanted them to develop their abilities and pursue activities that would enhance and augment His creation.

As part of God's family, we have a unique opportunity to move beyond our own knowledge and limitations to pursue the excellence for which we were designed. Tomorrow is the land of opportunity, and today is the launching pad. God loves us and gave us an opportunity to take our lives and use them for His purposes. The possibilities are endless because we serve a limitless God.

WE ARE ONE IN THE SPIRIT UNTIL THERE ARE TWO!

PSALM 133

Turmoil! It's hard to think of a situation in life that's not associated with disagreement, discontent, and difficulty. It doesn't matter if you are at work, school, the mall, or just driving down the street. There is probably someone with whom you will come into conflict on any given day. Would that you could find a place of respite where people knew how to agree with one another and get along!

The church, that is, the body of believers, is supposed to be just such a place. It's a place where the needs and concerns of others are put before our own, a place where unity and harmony reign supreme, and where disunity and avarice are conspicuously absent. Well, that's the plan, but that's not how it often works out.

The obvious question is: why is this so? How is it that division and disagreement occur within the church? There are many answers to this question, the full discussion of which is far beyond the scope of these paragraphs. However, a few obvious issues come to mind that are worthy of discussion.

First, imbalances exist regarding our propensity to sin and the related overreaction to super-legalize the faith. All of us sin. This has been a given since Adam and Eve decided to augment their diet to include forbidden fruit. In today's church, this act would likely prompt a debate between those who would advocate for God's mercy toward individuals with a genetic weakness toward fruit-eating versus those who would advocate eliminating all fruit from one's diet entirely. Obviously both groups would be wrong, but it's likely neither would see it that way. Sadly the result would probably be to develop fruit and non-fruit denominations, each developing theological support for their fruit/non-fruit-based positions.

Second, there is pride, you know, good old-fashioned "my ideas are more important than yours" pride. The notion of superiority between individuals and groups goes back a long way. Throughout the scriptures, we see numerous examples of pride being the primary motivating factor for disagreements between people.

Third are style-based differences. Some of the problems caused by these disagreements come from simple personality differences among believers. Some individuals are very outgoing and demonstrative while others are more quiet and subdued. The problem arises when the two groups try to worship together. Some think true worship only happens with a great deal of enthusiasm and emotion, while their counterparts feel true worship only happens through reverence and a quiet spirit. The sad part is both groups are right, but they seldom listen to one another's ideas. God is a God of variety. You don't have to look too far to realize this. The reason others look different than we do is because God likes it that way. In short, God loves the worship of those who love Him. With Him, the heart of the believer matters more than the style.

God loves us in balance and in truth. He is not put off by our differences, but He is put off by our sin. It's our job to let go of the latter and embrace the former.

HOLIER THAN THOU: THE GREAT ICE MAKER

MATTHEW 12:22–37

How many people have we lost to the kingdom of Christ because of our pride in our piety? How many times have those who have reached out to the Lord been rejected by those who think they have a special insight into the faith? How many of us will the Lord hold responsible for causing the loss of one who would be saved? I think the answer to all three of these questions is the same: far too many!

It's sad, but all too often the longer we spend as church members, the more likely we are to be merciless and cold. We learn the right words to say and dress, get appointed to the influential boards, and even start teaching Sunday school. Unfortunately, somewhere in this process we begin to lose sight of where we came from and start to get caught up with ourselves. Instead of looking for opportunities to reach out to the lost, we begin making rules and regulations to insulate ourselves from those who either don't believe or refuse to practice the faith as we do. We say we subscribe to the gospel but deny access to it to those who don't meet our standards or violate one of our holy-sounding rules.

When someone is critical of us, we call them unscriptural on one extreme or religious zealots on the other. Sadly, the situation gets worse with age and time in service. Too often, the further we walk with the Lord, the less understanding and more dispassionate we become. Not once in His entire ministry did Christ reject someone for how they dressed, what they looked like, or the measure of their sin. His only test was openness to the gospel and a heart that desired God's love.

It's interesting, but this is not a new phenomenon. Christ faced the same problem during His time on earth as well. Have you ever noticed the ones Christ had the most problems with were the church leaders of His day? The government didn't bother Him, at least until the church leaders insisted Pilate murder Him. The common people flocked to hear His words, and sinners of all kinds were always welcome. Christ pointed out that it was not the healthy, but the sick who needed a doctor. Unfortunately, today the sick are often turned away at the door for being unhealthy, unpresentable, and unacceptable.

I am not making an argument against holiness. God told us to be holy because He is holy. I am making an argument against pride. Christ was perfectly holy, but He was never proud. Christ never sinned, but He spent the vast majority of His time with sinners, often subject to the criticism of church leaders. Christ forgave the sinner, even when caught in the act while the church leaders conspired to throw stones. There is a difference between standing up for the faith and being standoffish because of your faith.

We have to let go of our pride and bring the truth to the lost. We need to balance the call to holiness with the call to evangelize because those who need evangelizing are not currently holy. It's not a contradiction to be loving and compassionate while still being holy. Christ did it every day of His life. Isn't it time we did the same thing?

GIVING: ARE YOU SHOUTING OR WHISPERING?

MARK 12:41–44

Every Sunday it's the same: countless churches across the world pass the offering plate. Some do it with a flourish, others in silence, and still others almost with an apology. As the plate, basket, or other appropriately appointed receptacle makes its way down the aisle, people in the pews respond. Some give with great reverence, others with a great sense of duty, while some don't give at all. It's an interesting process beyond its simple mechanics because it demonstrates something about the participants, willing or otherwise.

In Mark 12:41–44, Christ is watching the process of giving to the Lord's work. He observes two different dimensions of giving. The first is a gift from abundance, while the second is a gift from a position of need. Jesus' concern and focus resided there. He was interested in motives and the condition of the giver's heart, not necessarily the size of the gift.

Now don't get me wrong. In both cases, Christ understands the benefit of the gifts to the church. Indeed, the realities of life require us to recognize there is a variety of giving abilities in the church. Christ taught, however, that there was another dimension to giving that is often lost in the process.

Giving is an indication of who we are and the condition of our hearts for God. Whether or not we give and the motives directing our giving illustrates our attitudes and passions as they relate to Christ and His church. Think of it this way: if you love someone with all of your heart, giving them a gift is a treat. You enjoy giving to them because it is an expression of your love. Additionally, when you're truly in love, you look for opportunities to give as an expression of your heart. Giving is fun and interesting. Moreover, the greater the size of the gift relative to your capability to give increases the intensity and sincerity of the act.

The woman Christ observed loved God and His church. She gave as an act of devotion and passion, looking for nothing in return. Those who preceded her gave for different reasons, but their level of sacrifice and commitment was measurably less. It's not that their gifts weren't appreciated; rather their involvement in their relationship to the Lord was more distant.

I don't think Christ was worried about balancing the church's budget. I also don't think He was concerned about the amount of the gifts. I think Christ wanted us to understand our giving reflects our heart for Him. It's not about the money as much as it is about our commitment to our relationship with Him. God created the universe. No amount of money we might acquire is going to be significant compared to the wealth already in God's hands. What God really wants is our heart, not just a small piece, but the whole thing. He wants to be dear to us. He wants us to offer Him all that we are.

The message here is simple. Giving is about your heart. How much of it are you willing to share with the Lord? If the dollars you offer to the Lord speak and each carried an "I love you" from your heart, would they be heard from across the room, or would they only amount to a small whisper?

THE CHURCH IS ALWAYS OPEN, EXCEPT WHEN IT IS NOT

MATTHEW 15:1–20

You pass them as you drive through town. They are usually nice buildings with well-maintained landscaping. The signs out front typically sport a catchy phrase or sly play on words designed to get your attention and make you think. Often there is an open invitation to "come in and join us this Sunday," followed by a listing of times when it would be advantageous to do so. It's a picture-perfect scene, perhaps not a Thomas Kinkade vision, but something that pulls at your heartstrings and compels you to walk inside.

You open the door, and the image you had in your mind merges with the setting lying before you. Warm lighting and regal colors converge, appealing to your sense of worship and awe. Moving slowly, you take a seat toward the back, close to the door through which you entered. Soon music starts. You hear familiar refrains of old hymns reaching to the very core of your being. You're glad to be in the house of the Lord. The preacher speaks, his tone authoritative yet kind. The message, while not fire and brimstone, conveys a sense of urgency to meet with the Lord and confront the shortcomings of your life. A challenge, a moment of prayer, and a final song close out the morning.

Your car moves down the highway, and you're looking for a place for lunch when it hits you. Something was missing. You review the morning. All of the pieces were there except no one spoke to you. No one said hello! Indeed, no one sat near you, and no one acknowledged you were even there. There were the obligatory visitor cards in the pew, but no one asked you to fill one out. Giving it more thought, you realize how uncomfortable you felt the entire time. You had missed the feeling until this moment because you had been caught up in the beauty of the surroundings. It was a nice place, but you don't feel motivated to go back.

Is an open church a building with the door unlocked, or is it the home of people who love the Lord and know how to reach out to others? Too often, we confuse one with the other. We focus too much on the trappings of worship and too little on the one being worshipped, not to mention those worshipping Him. This is a dangerous and counterproductive way of life. It is also a good way to chase people away from the faith rather than draw them to it. We can become too concerned that our worship fits a particular mold rather than determine how to remold those worshipping. That's precisely the problem Christ had with the church leaders of His day.

When Christ was negatively criticized during His ministry, oftentimes the critical people were Pharisees and Sadducees who saw themselves as more spiritual than most. These church leaders prided themselves on being models of perfection and holiness. The problem was that they were so caught up with themselves that the condition of their parishioners went largely ignored. Moreover, they objected to healing and blessings surrounding Christ's ministry, even though it directly benefitted the recipients. I'm not sure how it comes about that a church leader is offended by a miracle, but it happened. Still, it makes no sense.

All of this would be just an interesting story if similar things didn't continue to happen today. There is a growing tide within churches where more and more of them want to look like the beacon on the hill but become offended when someone turns on the light. They fancy themselves as having it all together because everything looks nice, but there is no depth to their faith. They are more concerned that the pastor's sermons are politically correct and do not exceed the requisite twenty minutes than what the message is about in the first place. Church to these people has become more about the packaging rather than the contents of the box.

Christ had a message to tell. He wasn't as concerned about where it was told as much as He was focused on impacting the hearts of those who heard it. The point was changing lives, not whether the change took place in a pretty building or that the service was conducted according to a well-planned script. Christ was focused on bringing people to the Father, not how they dressed for the occasion. He welcomed the sinner and tax collector, and He wasn't worried about how they looked or if they fit the mold. There is much more that could and maybe should be said, but I think you get the point. So let me simply say this: beware the church caught up with itself. It may be long on style, but short on grace.

SOME ARE PRE-TRIB, BUT WHAT IF GOD IS POST-TRIB?

MATTHEW 24

New revelations, astounding insights, hidden codes, such is the latest media frenzy. No longer is there an interest in the basic truths handed down to us through the generations; now we need to uncover the secret conspiracy overlooked for hundreds of years. We find our satisfaction today in uncovering the baser side of existence. Heroes of bygone years are torn down by recently revised news of heretofore unknown evil deeds. Underlying it all is a subtheme that we can't trust our beliefs and that the history we once knew is nothing more than fiction designed to mislead.

"What is truth?" is a quote for the ages (John 18:38). It is the hope of everyone, whether they admit it or not, to know the truth, to understand the foundation upon which to base their lives. Absent truth, there can be no meaningful purpose in life. We can look for meaning in our careers, families, or friends, but without truth, there can be no lasting trust or depth.

The Bible tells us in the end times, truth will become an enigma. Deception will run rampant. Not only will social mores be questioned, but the very faith many base their lives on will be rocked by deceptions and false claims. While the Holy Spirit will be active, the enemy will also be busy attempting to deceive believers and non-believers alike.

While growing up, it was difficult to conceive of an age where reason would give way to misconception and misinformation. The world seemed very cut and dried, easy to understand, and well ordered. Now, things are quite different.

For years, I've had a concern that seems to be an increasingly likely scenario. What if Christ tarries about His return? What if the post-tribulation scenario is correct? The Bible tells us in the last days many will be deceived and fall away from the faith. Does this come about because of direct persecution or because the truth about the timing of a post-tribulation scenario is what actually occurs? Obviously the verdict regarding which interpretation of scripture is still out. My concern, however, is that the more painful post-tribulation scenario will ultimately prove to be correct.

If this is so, what of the people/believers who thought otherwise? Will it make it more likely for them to fall away from the faith if they have to live through times of persecution and torment, particularly if they didn't expect they would have to? I find this question quite troubling.

Christ told his disciples to prepare for persecution and hatred directed toward them for the faith they held dear, and they did not live through the tribulation period. Nonetheless, I believe the warning applies to us as well. Deception is on the rise at a time when people are increasingly uninformed about the truth of the gospel. Moreover, world events seem to point to storm clouds rising, just as they were predicted to do by Christ Himself. No man or woman knows the day or hour of Christ's return, but He will return. When He does, we will have either weathered the storm or have been swept away by it. The best advice I can give is to plan for a Category 5 and celebrate if you're gone before the first raindrops fall.

IF YOU'VE NEVER SHED A TEAR IN CHURCH, MAYBE YOU SHOULD TRY IT

2 CORINTHIANS 1:23–2:11

I grew up in a pretty stoic church. The services were nice, and the gospel was preached. The truth of God was revealed, but the emotional level did not vary much. Each Sunday held the promise of a good service, but there were few occasions of significant highs and/or lows.

The upside was that you could always count on the services to be very consistent. The downside was there were few occasions to deeply move your heart. Clapping was considered out of place, and no one ever raised their hands in praise.

I learned a lot in that church because the Bible teaching was good. I was saved there and learned the meaning of having a consistent Christian walk. It was church. It was formal. To me, however, something was missing, an element to my faith that my spirit truly craved.

Many years have passed since those early experiences. I went away to school and settled down with my wife in a city hundreds of miles from home. Over the ensuing years, I had the opportunity to attend several churches, not to mention the chapel services at college. During that time, I began to learn what I had been missing-emotion, in and about my faith. It's not that emotion was an end in and of itself; rather I learned that my relationship with Christ requires both emotional and intellectual elements.

In essence, I learned that my relationship with Christ was just that, a relationship. Accordingly, as any healthy relationship should, I decided knowing Christ required using both sides of my personality. Not only could I interact with Christ on an intellectual level, but I could also appeal to Him about and with my feelings. This opened up a whole new realm to me that I had not previously explored. I began to understand I could relate to Christ in essentially the same manner I did with anyone else I loved. Now when I felt moved to laugh, I could. When I felt moved to cry, I would. When I needed more understanding, I would ask. I began to relate more to the person of Christ with the full compliment of emotions and intellectual skills God gave me.

That is the key. I think we sometimes believe we have to strictly approach the Lord through some kind of formal arrangement. We're told to take our petitions to Him and confess our trespasses. These are important concepts, but they are often expressed exclusively through a formal context. The result is to consistently define our relationship with Christ on a very high level, all too often leaving out the depth of our feelings and concerns.

It's easy to overlook that Christ personally expressed a variety of emotions. The Scriptures tell us Christ was moved with compassion on several occasions when He reached out to heal a sick or dying person. "Jesus wept" (John 11:35). This, the shortest verse in the Bible, describes Jesus' reaction when he arrived at the home of Mary and Martha after Lazarus's death. Before he raised Lazarus from the dead, Christ showed He was greatly moved by the situation. Christ was not afraid to allow people to see His emotional side. It was part of who He was. Importantly, it is a part of who we are as well.

The key here is to approach Christ as we would anyone we truly love and respect. We must learn how to laugh and cry both to and with Him. We should communicate what is in our hearts to Him, including the soft and vulnerable parts. We're in a relationship with Christ. It has all the elements of an ordinary earthly relationship, plus a supernatural dimension not fully comprehensible in this life. In short, we need to be real with God. He already knows our hearts. It's just our turn to recognize it.

CHURCH PEOPLE AREN'T PERFECT; I KNOW BECAUSE I AM ONE

PSALM 6

One of the hardest things about being a Christian is actually being a Christian. I've known the Lord for the better part of my life, yet I still struggle with sin and temptation. You would think after all these years I would have this situation figured out, but the goal of holiness continues to elude me. To be honest, I tend to get frustrated over this problem and often wish I could walk in the footsteps of Christ just as He called me to do.

With all of the reading and studying I've done, not to mention discussions with a variety of other Christians, I've come to realize my situation is not unique. To date, I have yet to meet a Christian who does not struggle with the old self, also known as our sinful nature, even though they have had a valid salvation experience. I find this encouraging and discouraging all at the same time. I'm encouraged because I realize I'm not alone in my struggle with the temptations of this world. At least I can know others face similar problems as well. The discouraging part is realizing I will probably face similar trials over the balance of my life.

All right, so I struggle as do others. What's the point? The point is grace and forgiveness. The point is we are all losers absent Christ. In other words, we can attend church as much as we want, contribute all we have, dress right, and say all of the right things at just the right time and still come up short. We are Christians, meaning we are forgiven—not sinless, perfected in Christ, and not perfect in our own right.

There are a couple of problems with this situation, however. When we fall into sin, particularly conspicuous sin, the world sees us as hypocrites. After all, Christians are supposed to be good people, not given to sinful actions or vices. Moreover, too often when a fallen Christian attempts to repent, they are rejected as being irredeemable or untrustworthy. There is a lot of truth to the cliché that Christians tend to shoot their wounded. On the other hand, a few of us are so convinced of our own personal corner on holiness that we tend to be judgmental and cold. However it goes, these are problems we need to confront and overcome to improve Christ's message to this lost world.

While it's true we can't control the opinions of others, we can attempt to influence them. Accordingly, it's incumbent upon us believers to show the love of Christ to the world. Christ encouraged people to be holy by serving them and meeting their needs. Upon doing so, He had a basis from which He could communicate the truth. Christ loved people to the truth. He didn't beat them into submission.

As far as we're concerned, we must ever strive to approach our walk with humility and reverence. There is no room for a holier-than-thou attitude in the church. The Bible tells us, "all have sinned and fallen short of the Glory of God." (Romans 3:23, KJV) In a nutshell, that means believing yourself holier than the next guy proves you aren't. God judges, determines holiness, and sees our hearts. Unfortunately, holiness doesn't come to us naturally. That's why we need the supernatural gift of grace.

I'm saved by grace, and while I strive to accomplish good things, the accomplishments never negate the shortcomings. Yes, I'm a Christian who's trying to walk the walk and talk the talk. In the end, however, it doesn't make me perfect; nor does it make me better. It just makes me forgiven.

IF GOD IS WITH ME 24/7, WHY DO I FEEL SO ALONE?

PSALM 40

Life can be overwhelming. It's as simple as that. We all face difficulties, trials, and challenges that test our faith and tenacity. Most of us have the courage and fortitude to face each new day and the challenges accompanying it. What do we do, however, when we begin to feel like we are going it alone? I have to confess that even though I have known the Lord most of my life, at times He seems terribly far away. I feel somehow detached and aloof, cast adrift with no focus or direction. Working through those times is difficult, as I seem to become more keenly aware of my shortcomings and inadequacies. To be honest, I hate those days.

I have a wonderful family and good friends, and I am involved in many activities at church and in the community. All of these keep me busy, and I often find myself running to catch up with my relentless schedule. Yet, in the midst of all of this, I often get the feeling of being alone, terribly alone. I feel at those times that even though I'm busy and know a lot of people, I really am not known for who I truly am. Moreover, when my schedule overwhelms me and/or I come up short on a commitment, I begin to wonder if I'm really becoming the person God designed me to be. I look for God in my day, but sometimes He seems conspicuously absent. It makes my heart ache, and I begin to worry.

Interestingly, I don't think I'm unique in this perspective. When I read the Psalms, I note a large number of them address this problem, which brings me to the following realization: aloneness and loss are common feelings shared by believers and unbelievers alike. The difference for the believers is that we have a place to turn. We can turn to God. Still, what happens when we turn there and it seems He's out for the day?

The answer, I have found, is not necessarily simple. Well, perhaps it is, but it may not seem so. The answer is faith. The answer is, believing the

Bible and all of its promises about God's love for you actually apply to you. It's coming to the understanding God actually intends to be involved in your life personally and intimately. It means reaching out past your sense of aloneness to grasp the reality of an ever-present Father who loves you. You have to decide God really cares and fix your life and heart on it.

Faith is not a senseless belief in a fiction that will never come to be. It is not a delusional baseless pretense. Faith is knowing and accepting the truth and living life from the perspective that God is ultimately in control. Faith is applying the belief system taught in the Bible to your daily life in ways that give you the ability to risk and work for the Lord when circumstances suggest all is lost.

Finally, focus on God's love, not just in general but for you personally. For several years now, the Lord has been impressing on my heart that I should do this. I believe He wants me to understand the personal and intimate nature of His feelings for me. I believe He wants me to know His love is not an esoteric theory; rather it is a very real and tangible thing. I've learned I am capable of experiencing God's love by slowing down and meditating on His word. I know God loves me when I agree with the Holy Spirit that the Bible's promises truly apply to me. God's love is for me. God made that promise and decision long before I came on the scene. The promise is true. I just have had to learn to apply it to myself.

God does love you. You really are not alone. If you have accepted Christ as your Savior, He will always be at your side. You just have to decide to accept it.

WHY ISN'T THE CHURCH THE FIRST PLACE WE LOOK FOR EXEMPLARY BUSINESS PRACTICES?

DEUTERONOMY 25:13–16

I've always understood our responsibility as Christians was to be the individuals who would set the example of making a positive difference in the world. I thought we would be the ones who would consistently treat people well and deal honestly with them. Moreover, when it came to our employees, we would be the ones to go the extra mile to pay an above-average wage and see to their ancillary needs. I thought we would be the best at personnel development and providing a positive and warm work environment. The unfortunate truth is that all too often it just isn't so.

I've worked in the secular world for over twenty-eight years, and during that time, I've made some observations about my ministry-employed counterparts that I find to be dramatically disturbing. Frequently, my friends employed by churches and Christian ministries are treated poorly by their employers, underpaid relative to their secular counterparts, and expected to labor far beyond normal work hours to keep their positions. Sadly they are often told their sacrifice of wages, benefits, training, and respect is part of their sacrifice for the ministry. I'm not sure of the scriptural basis of this position, but it seems to be prevalent.

The problem goes beyond personnel issues, however. Many ministries are poor performers relative to the quality of service they offer, and they tend to be unreliable providers. It's also been my experience that too many Christian organizations are poor stewards of the resources they have been given, not to mention all too likely to be late paying their bills.

The Bible spends a lot of time talking about how we are to deal with one another, both from a faith-based and business perspective. Christ made it clear that Christians should be shrewd, kind, prompt, creative, conscientious, and fair. Importantly, He was not just interested in our personal lives, but our professional lives as well. He never taught there was a difference between personal and business ethics. Moreover, the Lord Himself taught the worker is worth his due. He lived by the Old Testament law, saying He did not come to refute the law, but to confirm it.

We have a mandate from the Lord to be exemplary individuals. Our lives stand as living testimonies to our faith in God and the true impact He has had on our lives. If people who deal with us have a difficult time discerning the faith we claim, do we really have faith? If people don't want to deal with us because we can't be relied upon to keep our word or defend the truth, do we have a valid witness?

Essentially we cannot make excuses, even if we wrap them in scripture verses, for not exceeding the world's standards in any part of our lives. We cannot claim to be valid witnesses for Christ if our business dealings show us more to be scoundrels and thieves. We have not only the responsibility, but the calling to be righteous, fair, courteous, compassionate, prudent, and kind in all of our dealings. Our Father calls us to excellence. The question is: will we strive for it?

THE PHARISEES GOT OFFENDED A LOT TOO

MATTHEW 12:1–14

"And he calls himself a Christian!" "We've gone to this church for three generations, and I'm not going to put up with this!" "All they ever talk about is money; this is a church, not a business!"

Sound familiar? Have I hit close to home? It's fairly likely if you've spent any time at all at church, particularly if you've served on a committee, that you've heard statements like those above. It's sad actually, but it seems too many of us have too many reasons for becoming offended by something or someone in the church. We're sensitive to the things that don't go our way or the people who don't fit our mold of what a Christian should do or say. We take issue with people who don't line up with us on all doctrinal issues and too often are quick to condemn or discount their potential contribution to the body of Christ.

Now, I recognize there are times when it's necessary to stand up and defend the faith. Indeed, the Bible teaches us that a trait of God's workers is that they are known for "rightly dividing the word of truth" and defending it wherever they are (2 Timothy 2:15). What I'm concerned with here is the propensity too many of us have for finding fault with others or being so intolerant of differing views on scripture that we cannot lovingly discuss the issues. There is a difference between misinterpreting scripture and trying to get a handle on issues upon which the Bible is particularly vague.

I believe much of the church's problem with offense has to do with the pride we all fight as human beings. Most of us tend to have difficulty accepting change of any kind. Additionally, some of us simply insist on being in control or being right about everything.

OK, so why did I stir up this can of worms? Simple. I don't believe our being offended on God's behalf is appropriate the majority of the time. Too often we are more attuned to our own sensitivities rather than issues the

Lord might find offensive. This is the difference between being godly and self-righteous. Obviously, we want the former but not the latter.

Additionally, it strikes me that Christ spent very little of His time being offended, and the ones most likely to offend Him or be offended by Him were the church leaders. Consider this passage in Matthew. The church leadership got offended with Christ. It was particularly troubling that they were increasingly offended when He did something good. If you take a step back, it doesn't make very much sense. In fact, it's quite absurd. Nevertheless, not only did they ignore the benefit of the miracles Christ performed, they were put off by the power of God being displayed in a manner they didn't appreciate. These were the church leaders being offended by the very God they claimed to serve. It doesn't make any sense until you factor in human pride and self-righteousness.

I take all of this as a warning to those of us who believe. It's easy to fall into a prideful trap that prevents us from effectively ministering on behalf of Christ. When we allow this to occur, we inhibit the Holy Spirit's work in this world, and we are offending the God we claim to serve. Simply put, look for reasons to be loving and compassionate rather than excuses to be offended. If you do this, you'll be much more effective at expanding the kingdom.

HOLINESS AND LEGALISM ARE NOT THE SAME THINGS

MATTHEW 15:1–20

Don't go to movies. Don't play cards. Don't drink. Don't smoke. Don't cuss. Don't … Don't … Don't … Oh, and by the way, guys should always wear suits to church, and the ladies must always wear dresses. There are a large number of other rules as well, and we will advise you of what they are as we go along and/or as we think them up!

And we wonder why people are not easily motivated to go to church and experience a saving relationship with Christ. The answer is obvious. Instead of offering them forgiveness of sins and an opportunity to know peace and joy in their lives, we inflict upon them rules and regulations designed to cause them to toe the line and live up to our standards. The problem is that our standards vary from church to church, and many do not even appear in Scripture. Where there is a grey area in Scripture, we augment its teachings with hard and fast rules, allowing no room for error or opposition. We like to make new rules for others to follow so they can attain the same level of spiritual maturity we believe we have attained ourselves.

Christ calls us to salvation via His grace. Obviously there should be a change of heart at the point of salvation. It should be evident to others Christ has made a difference in our lives. We should be motivated by love and humility, seeking to bless others with God's abundant mercy. There should be marked differences between our behavior and the behavior of those who don't know Christ. We should tend toward holiness out of love for our Savior, living our lives after His example.

There is a difference, however, between living a do/don't do list and seeking a closer relationship with the Father because of our love for Him. Do and Don't lists become empty exercises over time. Instead of focusing us on our Lord, they often become the focal point themselves. When the

Pharisees complained about Christ's followers' hand washing, they were not interested in their hygiene as much as they were looking for faults and shortcomings. Instead of wanting to lead the disciples into a closer walk with the Father, they were fishing for a reason to condemn and demean them. In their own eyes, the Pharisees saw themselves as more perfect, more holy, and more spiritually mature than anyone else. Their preoccupation with their own power and position prevented them from truly serving God and recognizing the Messiah Himself when He stood right in front of them.

Christ was intent upon saving the lost and didn't require them to become perfect before they could hear the truth. He encouraged holiness out of a loving heart and did not invoke a perfection contest in the process. We are called to be holy and seek a closer walk with Christ. This is achieved by acting on the love we can have in our hearts for our Savior who died to redeem us. Even though we are called to be holy, we can only be saved by grace. Therefore, living the do/don't do list won't benefit us. It's our hearts that need to change.

WHAT TO DO WHEN A CHRISTIAN LETS YOU DOWN

PSALM 133

People aren't perfect, although I have to admit I wish they were. Over the years, I've had many friends, and it's a blessing to know the vast majority of them are Christians. Christianity creates a common bond among people that gives them the ability to find mutual understanding and perspective on life. It provides a significant foundation for mature and lasting relationships that have the ability to grow deep and strong.

Friendships are not without their risks, however. All of us are different people. We have our likes and dislikes, and we react to situations differently. My experience as a Christian has been that difficulties and disagreements with other Christians are even more painful and more difficult to manage. I believe this occurs because faith becomes the basis for our perspective on the world. When disagreements occur between Christians, the love they share through Christ is bruised, at least potentially. Moreover, Christians tend to justify these positions by using some scriptural principle, all too often in a somewhat cutting way.

Honestly, these disagreements hurt. They divide and disappoint. Sometimes they drive a wedge between people that's difficult to remove. But remove it we must.

I'm not going to suggest that there is a simple A-B-C kind of response to this problem because there isn't. Real problems between people are not resolved with some cookie-cutter answer that is too shallow to do anything but cause more harm. Rather the solution is a combination of several elements starting with love and forgiveness. True love between individuals requires a lot of hard work. It takes years to cultivate. While compromise is a worthy alternative, often the solution is more complicated. Occasionally the two parties have to agree to disagree and learn to manage their relationship around the issue or problem. Christ understood that impasses would occasionally arise between people in general and His people in particular. He encouraged us as much as possible to live peacefully with all men (Romans 12:18).

As Christians, we should get along with people and do our best to love the disagreeable. We also need to realize the road to friendship is not an easy one. People, Christian or not, are people. They are not perfect and will not be perfect in this lifetime. They need your forgiveness as much as you need theirs. Loving one another requires considerable effort. It doesn't come easy, but it is an important component of our Christian calling. We need to keep in mind that we cannot make the other person approach relationships or life issues the way we do. The result then is that different positions, ideas, and personalities exist all around us. They don't evaporate when we meet Christ. So stay with it. Recognize people are imperfect and respond accordingly. Finally, remember you're not perfect either. Someday it will be your turn to be forgiven.

IT REALLY IS AMAZING GRACE

EPHESIANS 2:1–10

I wish I could tell you that I deserve to write this message. I wish I could tell you I am beyond blemishes and scars. I wish I could tell you that I am the perfect church member without fault or wrinkle. I wish I could tell you, but I can't. So I won't because it's not true.

When I consider all of the sins and shortcomings of my life, it becomes hard to believe that God would consider loving me, let alone saving me. But He does and He did. I look at my life, and it's easier to enumerate my faults and sins than come up with reasons I should receive eternal life, but I have it. It was a gift.

If you honestly and dispassionately look at your life, you will realize how short you fall from God's perfection. I don't point this out as a put down to insult you. I'm simply recognizing the cold hard facts as I see them. Any way you cut it, none of us are perfect. What's worse, it doesn't matter if we try to do nice things. We can't obscure our imperfections.

That, however, is the whole point. We have received a gift. If we could earn our salvation, we would be receiving a reward or payment for our deeds. Nothing we can do is good enough to overcome the debt we owe. We have incurred a debt that far exceeds our ability to pay. What's more, we will be judged against a perfect law that allows no room for error. Therefore, since we cannot even come close to repaying our debt, we are in need of someone to come to meet this obligation for us. That person is Jesus Christ.

It's striking how many people find it difficult to accept this simple truth. It seems so often that people believe they have to earn their way to heaven as if their personal efforts are sufficient to overcome their personal mountain of debt. Plain and simple, it can't be done. What's so beautiful about God's plan through Christ is that it's so easy to do. Moreover, anyone can understand it, and anyone can do it.

So what holds people back? Personally I believe it's one of several things: pride, guilt, misunderstanding, misdirection, and mistrust are a few that come to mind. I'm sure there are many more. Essentially many are passing up the opportunity to know the Lord for reasons that make little or no sense from the perspective of eternity. We all need to understand the Lord wants to enjoy a relationship with us. He is not sitting on a big throne somewhere looking for the next chance to zap us for doing something we shouldn't. Neither is He an indifferent force casually looking on as the world passes us by. God is a personal Creator who loves His creation, more specifically, us. He was heartbroken at the fall of man, and He set about to redeem us to Himself in a way that wouldn't compromise His perfection. He came up with the perfect solution, the perfect gift, Jesus Christ.

We could never have deserved such consideration; nor could we have overcome our loss. Rather God chose to give the best and most perfect gift, His Son. That God gave this gift is amazing. That He gave it for me is astounding. That He gave it for us is astonishing. Amazing Grace, it is the sweetest sound!

I DO LOVE THE LORD; I JUST WANT TO DO IT BETTER

ROMANS 7

I wish I had known Paul. He was probably a pretty great guy. He was honest, he was driven, and he practiced his faith vigorously and passionately. The thing I like the most, I think, was his human nature. Paul was not caught up with himself. He didn't spend a lot of time bragging or accusing people of all kinds of problems. He was a great leader and pastor, but he never became a tyrant. Most importantly, he wasn't afraid to admit his sinful side existed. He wasn't perfect - even orchestrating the deaths of Christians. (I think it's fair to say that this was probably not an attribute that would endear him to any pastoral search committee.)

Paul was imperfect, even flawed, but above all, he loved the Lord. As such, he has become an increasingly important example for me. You see, I'm flawed too. I struggle with the same kinds of issues Paul spoke about. I know the difference between right and wrong and can usually tell what I should be doing. Yet even though I know how I should act or think, I still find myself wanting to do the wrong thing. I can directly relate to this passage Paul wrote, particularly verses 14–20. How often I've felt just the way Paul described. It's frustrating!

Now I don't want you to think that I sit around looking for ways to get in trouble. I know how I should behave. It's just that I hate having to deal with temptation! It goofs up my day and requires way too much energy. Life would be so much simpler if we didn't have to deal with things of the world that distract us from our walk with Christ. I just wish I could focus more of my life on my relationship with Him than I do now. But that's the point, isn't it?!

We have but a few years here on earth before we go to be with the Lord. Within those years, we need to find Christ as our Savior, learn the truths of His word, and apply His teachings to our actions. It's simple really, at least until the adversary finds out. Then the trouble starts. I have learned something about my struggles with sin. It's not just the sin that has a price, but also the time the sin robs me of that I could have used achieving God's goals for my life. I know I have to consider right and wrong, but I also need to be aware of the minutes, hours, and days lost to fruitless desires.

In short, I only have so many years on this planet within which to live out my life for Christ. Every moment is precious. I just need to treasure the time more directly. In other words, if I focus more of my daily activities on Christ and His direction for my life, I will enjoy a fuller, more balanced existence.

Every day represents an opportunity to honor the Lord and enhance our relationship with Him. In Revelation, the Lord tells us that He wants us to be either hot or cold toward Him. In other words, don't be a fence sitter. Make the call to be devoted to the Lord. Become passionate about your relationship with Him and pursue Him with all of your energy. We live in a world that competes for our affection and attention. We can't afford to be passive about our faith. We need to turn up the heat and warm up to the Savior who loves us.

WHAT IF IT COSTS US EVERYTHING?

PHILIPPIANS 1

B argains! We're always looking for bargains. We listen for ads on TV telling about the latest sales on the best merchandise. Open up the Sunday paper, and you find an entire section devoted to telling us where to find the best deals on every need we can imagine. And don't forget to clip those coupons!

Our society is increasingly focused on reducing the cost of everything. Much of this activity is good because it simply teaches us to be more efficient and effective with the limited resources we have. Moreover, we learn to be respectful and mindful of the cost of everything we do.

Unfortunately there is a related problem with this situation as well. We tend to be frugal in areas where it is actually detrimental to do so. Instead of devoting the time and energy necessary to succeed, we economize resulting in disappointment and failure. Some areas of our lives actually require us to infuse lavish amounts of effort to achieve the desired results. Consider your relationship with your spouse, children, friends, and colleagues, not to mention your education, physical training for a task, or focusing on your talent or unique ability.

Some things in this life beg for our attention beyond a casual level of interest; they require a level of devotion and attention bordering on obsession to gain the results we desire. For example, if you are attempting to woo the love of your life to marry you, you will put every effort into accomplishing the task. You will look for opportunities to please, find excuses to give gifts, and spend every waking hour thinking of ways to make them happy. Importantly, the task will be pleasant, and the time, effort, and resources you spend will seem a minor trade for the prize you seek.

So what about Christ? Where does He fall on the spectrum of cost/

benefit in our lives? When we think about our relationship with Him, is it more akin to clipping coupons or lavishing gifts on the one we love? Do we spend every waking moment looking for ways to please Him and walk more closely to Him, or do we merely allocate a few quality moments to Him in our day timer? Are we excited about the next opportunity to get together with Him, or is He reduced to an obligation to be accommodated when we get around to it?

Loving Christ is an all-encompassing way of life. Living with and for Him should be based on a complete focus of our time and energy. Our relationship with Him should bring us joy, and we should be overwhelmed with anticipation about our next encounter. Finally we should be willing to pay the cost of our devotion to Him. In a world increasingly hostile to the gospel and Christ in particular, we need not only to be aware of the cost of our love but also welcome the opportunity to pay it. Nothing worthwhile is free, and our relationship with Christ is more than worthwhile. Though it may cost us everything, we should live for Christ and shout about our devotion from the mountaintops!

"TIS SO SWEET TO TRUST IN JESUS," BUT MUCH OF THE TIME I DON'T

PSALM 55

I don't know about you, but I have times in my life when I feel out of sorts and off balance. It's not necessarily that things are falling apart as much as they are simply not coming together. It seems during these periods the enemy attacks me more and I find myself feeling overwhelmed and alone. These are days when I'm in the doldrums—no mountaintops and no deep valleys. I can see those places from where I am, but they're not close. The days are like cars in a passing freight train; each passes through my view, but none is so distinct as to stir my emotions and passions.

Life is strange. We're encouraged to plan and achieve, seek great opportunities, and live life at the mountaintop. Yet in the actual process, life is much more tame and routine. It's in the routine where we tend to run into the greatest obstacles and experience the hindrance of the mundane.

Certainly we all experience happy times and sad, positive and negative, exciting and boring. Most of these are short lived; in between we find ourselves trying to figure out how to make it to the next great experience. The questions are: how do we live out the days that last forever? How do we move through the flatland moments?

There is an answer to this question that is, of course, obvious, but in so being is often overlooked: Jesus. It's funny-we find it easy to look to Him when we're at the end of our rope. We also tend to remember to thank Him for the wonderful times and give Him the praise He deserves. But how do we approach Christ when things are just passing us by without much fanfare or bravado?

I believe it's important for us to learn to bring Christ into our lives even when we don't feel a great sense of emotion or direction. During the mundane times, we need to remind ourselves that Christ is neither passionless nor indifferent about anything going on in our lives. We must consider that the one who created us is acutely focused on us and the events of our lives. There is nothing that can possibly happen in our world that doesn't fascinate our Lord.

Trusting in Jesus doesn't just apply to the pinnacles and trenches. It applies to the daily routine of our lives as well. It doesn't matter that we can't personally muster the enthusiasm we should have for the day at hand. God is passionate about everything that comes our way. The trick is reminding ourselves that God wants to be with us even when we're not good company or particularly worked up about our present situation.

THE GOSPELS NEVER SAY, "AND CHRIST SHOUTED," SO WHY DOES THE PREACHER?

MATTHEW 5:1–20

I've heard it said that a preacher often shouts the loudest about the point in his sermon he can support the least. The funny thing is that the statement is too often true. I'm not a preacher, but I do teach, and I can understand the assertion. It's hard to bring a message about Christ that's fully consistent and timely, that will catch the hearts and minds of the people in the room. Also people like to know what they are doing is relevant and inspiring. Preachers are people too, and the temptation to prove their own personal worth can hit them right between the eyes.

It has been two thousand years since Christ walked this earth. Much has changed, but much remains the same. Human nature is pretty consistent today with what was evident in Christ's day. Christ understood this in His teaching. He wasn't afraid to tell the truth and let the chips fall where they may. Indeed His words often cut to the heart of the matter regardless of His audience. Many loved and revered Him, yet an important group, by and large, did not - the church leaders. They had fallen prey to the deception of position and pride. Their messages no longer resonated with the love of God for the people. Rather they brought a message that fostered their own personal agendas and positions. They were more concerned with maintaining the status quo than ushering people into the presence of God. They claimed to be looking for the Messiah, but they completely overlooked Him when He looked them square in the eye.

Christ brought the truth. He did not vary from it; nor did He complicate it. He wasn't worried that His words were eloquent; nor was He concerned whom they might offend. When there were people in the crowd who openly objected or opposed Him, He remained direct and nonplussed. Above all, He was always level. He didn't rely on overarching methods; nor did he attempt to intimidate. He was clearly the leader, but He never became aloof or out of touch. Furthermore, He extended His reach to those society deemed too far gone or simply unimportant.

Christ was passionate about His ministry here on earth. He devoted His full efforts to His task, aggressively pursuing His Father's purposes. Yet in all His time preaching, He never seemed to project an image of being more important than those He loved. Importantly, He brought His messages out of a spirit of love and concern for those who would hear them. Christ didn't try to intimidate because He relied on the truth to touch the hearts of the people. The truth doesn't have to be force-fed; it stands on its own merit. Truth may be questioned, but it will always stand the test.

Christ didn't shout because He had the right message. This in itself is a lesson to us: separate the bravado from the words. Check the basis of the sermon against the truth of Scripture. If the message has merit, it will ring true, regardless of the volume with which it was delivered.

THE AXIOM "THERE ARE NO ABSOLUTES" IS AN OXYMORON!

PROVERBS 4

Contradictions demand resolution. If one is to have a rational purpose for doing anything, they must produce defensible criteria upon which a solid foundation can be built. Attempting to support a line of reasoning absent logical truths is folly, subjecting the individual to ridicule and ultimate failure. Moreover, basing one's life on a false assumption or position renders an existence of meaninglessness and hopelessness.

A position that became popular in the past generation, "There are no absolutes," has become the rallying cry of many who would deny the existence of God and His Son, Jesus Christ. The two positions tend to walk hand in hand. If God does not exist, there is no basis for absolute truths because there is no one with the power or authority to establish such truths. Furthermore, if you desire to define your own terms for your existence or provide a foundation for setting up your own morals outside the bounds of those existing within society and/or the church, denying the veracity of absolutes is essential.

From the moment Adam and Eve fell in the garden, human beings have attempted to invent their own social mores exclusive of God's directives. As a result, definitions of right and wrong have meandered around a continuum between good and evil. Those societies that have attempted to adhere to the absolutes contained in the Bible have had far greater success and been foundational to improving society and quality of life in general. Those who have strayed from biblical absolutes have ultimately degenerated into self-consuming people groups, becoming either inconsequential or extinct.

The very notion that there are no absolutes is a contradiction on its very face. The statement itself must be an absolute in order to hold in all situations. Unfortunately the statement cannot be an absolute by the very content of the statement itself. Sadly, people still attempt to base their lives on this proposition because they perceive such a position affords them the freedom to pursue positions on morals of their own design that may or may not be consistent with their own or others' best interest. Ultimately, this indefensible position results in anarchy and destroys the foundation of society and the life of the individual.

The Bible establishes moral truths designed to promote love and harmony between people. Moreover, it provides a framework whereby human beings can organize socially and achieve all God designed them to do. Our tendency as sinners is to throw off the apparent restrictions God gave us in His word. Importantly, we are the happiest and encounter the least number of problems when we do conform our lives and opinions to the guidance our loving Father gave us in His word.

IF IT'S NOT CONSISTENT, DROP IT!

GALATIANS 2

There are many messages in the world today. We are being challenged on every front regarding issues that used to be obvious and clear. Not only are long-held moral standards being questioned, but Christian truths are being watered down and bent over to accommodate popular ideas. No longer are our children being given consistent guidelines for growth and maturity. Relativism has become the order of the day, and the dictates of appropriate behavior change as frequently as the headlines.

Much of what is happening should not be a surprise to most Christians. The Bible foretells perilous times and confusion about social mores. As we approach Christ's return, more and more problems will arise, challenging the very fabric of our faith. Sadly, we are told that many will fall away from the faith as they are drawn to false teaching or succumb to social pressure. Times will become more difficult from here, particularly for Bible-believing Christians seeking to stand for the truth of the gospel.

It's not time to despair or lose hope. It is time to know the truth and stand on it. The problem of dealing with misleading perspectives or teachings is not a new one. Paul encountered similar problems during his ministry. Of particular interest is the fact that some of those who fell prey to false teaching, legalism, and political pressure were some of the original disciples. This is notable not because of the level of faith or devotion of the individual, rather because it illustrates the fact that anyone can fall.

None of us get a pass on having to deal with discerning the truth from fiction. All of us have the responsibility to gain a good working knowledge of the foundational truths of our faith to reduce the likelihood of finding ourselves on the wrong side of important issues. Furthermore, we need to have the intestinal fortitude to do what is right based on biblical principles rather than what's popular. We need to pay attention to the warning flags waving in our heads when someone tells us they have a new revelation from God.

God revealed His truth to us through His word. The message is consistent and clear, without contradiction. When read in context, the Bible is full of foundational teaching providing the basis for living a full and rewarding life and providing the way to salvation through Jesus Christ. The advantage of the truth is that it doesn't change with the times or the latest fad. Political expediency is not on the agenda; neither are popular sensitivities.

We have a responsibility to be ever watchful, ever guarded. When it comes to the truth, we have a mandate to be immovable and firm. While compassion and mercy are part of our calling, we are not called to compromise our faith to touch other lives. Test what you hear and what you learn. Keep the teachings consistent with the Bible; cast off the rest.

GOD IS LORD OF ALL, AND HE DOESN'T NEED YOUR PERMISSION

PSALM 24

God is Lord of all. It's probably safe to say all true Christians subscribe to this declaration. Few of us would argue God is only Lord of certain things, like Nebraska, for instance. It should be obvious on its face that accepting God as sovereign over all of the earth and the universe is consistent with the Scripture. Furthermore, if we truly believe God is who He says He is, that He has created all we know and see, we shouldn't have a problem accepting the dimensions of His power and authority. Giving God credit for creating us and accepting His lordship over our lives should be a natural thing. Unfortunately, we often live contrary to the notion of God's authority in our lives.

We live in a world confronting us about the veracity of our faith. Important issues from the question of the existence of God Himself to the sanctity of the human life He created are heatedly debated. The media scoffs at conservative Christian values as being out of date, bigoted, or irrelevant. Children are not permitted to pray at school, and faculty members are admonished for sharing their Christian beliefs. Such is the secular world.

Unfortunately, the challenges to our faith extend to our churches as well. Many Christian churches have some level of difficulty accepting the Bible as the infallible Word of God. Important issues such as those enumerated earlier suffer under Christian-colored political sensitivity and fall to the mores of the day. Life is no longer sacred. Beliefs of false religions are tolerated as alternative ways to get to God contrary to the teachings of Scripture.

All of this seems to make believing in God very complicated and difficult. Tolerance and blind compassion dictate acceptance of ideas obviously opposed to biblical teachings. The real truth is that believing in God is simple. The Word of God is true, and while some study is required, it is readily understandable. The black-and-white issues in the Bible related to how we can know Christ and how we should live remain unchanged. Moreover, while some grey area issues exist, the underlying principles for how to deal with them are available for our instruction.

In my experience, the most common reason for individuals to leave the true teachings of Scripture and embrace erroneous positions is simply pride. We want to fit in and be seen as worldly-wise and astute. We want to be sensitive; a good trait we should cultivate, but we choose unwise methods for doing so. Our desire to get along and fit in overrides the true instruction of the Word, resulting in a watered-down faith full of apologies for what is truly right and good.

The Bible teaches that in the final days many will fall away from the faith. In many instances, this will probably happen because of the outright conflict between Christian and societal moral values. The temptation is to succumb to societal mores in the name of tolerance and compassion. While conventional wisdom might dictate going with the crowd, the underlying risk is abandonment of the truth of God for the flawed values of society at large.

God provided guidance to us about how we should live our lives. The guidance is contained in a book called the Bible. The Bible is not a collection of nice ideas carrying varying degrees of importance for incorporation into our behaviors. It is the infallible word of God. God is the Creator of all that is. He is sovereign. He is Lord, and with all due respect, He doesn't need your permission to exist, to express Himself, or to dictate what is right and wrong.

WISHING IT WERE SO RAISES THE POSSIBILITY!

PSALM 33

Put your hope in the Lord. We must realize our provision for life and the possibilities of tomorrow rest with God. It is easy in this day and age to become discouraged and lose the ability to dream. We suffer setbacks or listen to others who have, and we begin to accept the status quo instead of seeking something more. This is contrary to the Lord's purposes for us. Beginning with Adam and Eve, God has always encouraged His people to be creatively involved in the world. Additionally He wants us to learn to look to Him when the odds seem stacked against us or when our circumstances seem to limit life's possibilities.

All of us face hurdles in our lives. We are met with challenges from the day we are born. We all have to learn to walk, talk, dress, and carry on a daily routine that becomes second nature by the time we are two years old. As we grow, we enter school and meet new challenges as we learn concepts and skills that will carry us through the rest of our lives. Along the way, some of the lessons we learn come with some frustration and difficulty, but in the end, we are better for it, and we grow.

Unfortunately something happens when we become adults. We find it increasingly difficult to take on new challenges or reach out toward exciting opportunities. Instead of being inspired to try our hand at something new, we rest on our past successes and become satisfied to move no further. In time, we become discouraged and find life to be monotonous and dull.

I would like to submit to you that life is anything but dull and the possibilities for your life are limited only by your desire to achieve and ability to learn. The Lord created each of us for a purpose, a purpose matched to the desires of our hearts, gifts, and talents. The important thing for us to remember is our abilities, desires, and talents are raw materials. You may want to play the violin and may have a natural ability for music, but unless you practice and suffer through mistakes and a time of poor technique, you will never master the art.

The possibilities in our life are more often limited by the measure of our willingness to endure the learning process and overcome the setbacks than lack of potential. Regardless of your age, you can have dreams. You can be optimistic about the potential of your future within God's plan. The important thing is not to lose the ability to dream. You need to believe not only that God loves you, but that He is supporting and encouraging you to achieve all He designed you for.

Very few people achieve success because the opportunities fall at their feet all at once. Most people are confronted with a problem or challenge they become motivated to address. The opportunity comes as part of doing something about a potential adverse event. Other times, dreaming about what could be provides the chance to realize a benefit where none existed previously. In either case, abiding hope is the foundation stone for realizing new achievements, achievements that may never have been if someone somewhere hadn't dared to dream.

ALTAR CALLS SHOULD BE FOR MORE THAN JUST NEW CHRISTIANS

JOHN 21:15–19

We need moments of intimacy in our lives. We need to share in depth who we are and what we are with someone who will love us regardless. Our souls were designed for an intimate relationship with our Father in heaven through our Lord and Savior Jesus Christ. The sad part is there are few opportunities within the context of a church experience for this to occur.

It is true we can share our lives intimately with the Lord anytime we choose. We can spend time reading His Word, praying, and meditating, all of which open opportunities to enjoy Him more. But what of those times at church when the music or sermon has been particularly moving? How do we approach the Lord more directly and physically?

For new Christians, an altar call is a time for adopting a new direction. It's a chance to take a stand for Christ by physically presenting oneself at the altar to become a person set apart for the Lord's service. For existing Christians, the opportunities to renew or reaffirm our faith tend to be fewer and farther between. Don't get me wrong. There are many altar calls for those who have backslidden, lost their way, or become caught up in the ways of the world. How often, however, do we have altar calls just to enjoy the presence of the Lord and share our love with Him?

I believe it would be healthy to design more time in our church experience to share some intimate moments with the Savior just because it's a pleasant thing to do. When Adam and Eve walked with the Lord in the garden before the fall, they were free to enjoy the company of the Father for the sheer pleasure of it. Their time together was joyful and peaceful. They had meaningful conversations and delighted in the achievements of the day.

We need to have the opportunity to share similar experiences with the Lord. Christ came into the world to redeem us unto Himself and to open the way to the Father. This implies that sharing intimacy with the Father through Christ is the intended purpose of our lives. Accordingly, fostering intimacy with the Father is an important function of the church.

Christianity is not a faith about concepts; it is a faith about relationships. The first is our relationship with the Father, and the second is our relationship with each other. We can work on our relationship with Christ in numerous ways, but we need to be focused on being intimate with Him. We need opportunities to present ourselves personally and publically. We need to do this in a context that doesn't presuppose a problem, but rather in a way that simply says, "Lord, I love you!"

Every day with the Lord represents a chance to know Him more. It's an opportunity to add depth and meaning to the relationship. It's time we added altar calls just to enjoy the Lord, just to enhance our experience with Him and our love for Him.

A REAL GIFT HAS NO STRINGS

MATTHEW 2:1–12

It's Christmastime. I have to tell you that it's my favorite time of the year. I love the beauty of the season, the extra joy I carry around in my heart, the music, the decorations, the church services, and the exchange of gifts. It is a time of the year that hints at what the world really could be like if people truly focused on love, peace, joy, and hope. Just imagine what the world would be like if we all left behind our petty differences and devoted ourselves to blessing our neighbors throughout the year in the same way we tend to do at Christmas!

When Christ came into this world, He became the most beautiful of all gifts ever given. He represented the love of God for His creation that provided an opportunity for reconciliation beyond the hopes and dreams of fallen mankind. He was God, Creator of all that is, in human form here to shed His blood for the salvation of the world. In Matthew 2:1–12, the story of the Magi coming to find Christ, worship Him, and present Him with gifts is told. Most of us are familiar with the account and include their visit as part of our Christmas observance, even though most recognize they may have arrived about two years after Christ's birth. Upon seeing the Christ child, the Magi presented Him with gifts recognizing both His royalty and prophesied mission and sacrifice for us. The Magi's gifts recognized the majesty of Christ, while Christ's gift recognized the mercy of God. His gift was unearned and underserved by any of its intended recipients, namely us.

We give gifts today remembering the most wondrous gift we ever received. At least that's how it's supposed to be. Unfortunately it doesn't always work out that way. All too often, gifts are given with some expectation of something being given back in return. It's become a competition of sorts to see what kind of response comes from our giving something to someone else.

Sadly this misses the whole point. The best gift given is the one with no expectation of anything received in return. The gift given to an individual who can't give anything back brings the greatest pleasure to the giver, not to mention being sweet in the sight of the Lord. Our joy in life comes most fully from the things we do for and give to others. God designed us that way, but it's up to us to discover it.

Life is not about giving to get something. Life is about sacrificing all you are for another. Christ came and set the example for all of us. He came to show His unfailing love by sacrificing His very life as a gift of love for all people. You and I are recipients of His gift. The question is: will we accept it and share it with others?

Christmastime is not the only season of giving; nor is it the only time we should love one another. Giving in the spirit of Christmas should endure the whole year through, and the only string should be a cord of love.

CHRIST DIDN'T COME TO WIN A POPULARITY CONTEST

LUKE 6:1–11

Standing up for what is right has never been easy nor popular. In fact, the temptation is to go with the status quo, following the path of least resistance wherever it may lead. Those who stand up for what's right are frequently criticized and often aggressively opposed. Today, decisions are made based upon opinion polls and political expediency. In fact, doing the right thing is often not even an alternative; it is often omitted because of high risk, exceptional cost, or societal oversensitivity.

Sadly, we live in a day and age where ridicule has replaced debate about whether issues are right or wrong. Indeed, in many cases, the concept of simple right versus wrong is considered too crass or insensitive to others' feelings to be eligible as an appropriate alternative. Now someone is allowed to believe, do, or say anything if they are sincere about it and it doesn't offend someone else's sensitivities. Oddly, there is one disturbing exception to this soft, fluffy world; that is, anything resembling the Christian faith is automatically suspect. Moreover, open hostility to such a position is considered appropriate and expedient.

The world is upside down. Today we make allowances for inappropriate behavior, formerly known as sins, and dismiss proclivity to live contrary to biblical ethics by inventing alternative lifestyles and redefining previously accepted mores. We quickly abandon the moral high ground because to claim it is considered presumptuous, overbearing, hypocritical, and arrogant. It's now difficult to stand up for what's right because no one knows what it is and they are fearful to define it.

Interestingly the problem is not a new one. Christ stood up for what was right in His day only to be confronted by the keepers of power who had a radically different agenda. In Christ's day, the church was not fulfilling its role of moral leadership. Instead it had become a political power base for zealots to illustrate their mastery of religious dogma, forfeiting any benefit to the society at large. Christ came to challenge the power seekers and turn the hearts of the people back to the God who both created and loved them.

I know some in the world today would point to the modern church and announce similar criticisms. Unfortunately, some of their critiques would be correct. The institution of the church is not perfect, but that is precisely the point. We are not perfect. That's why we need Christ as our Savior. Our imperfections should not be allowed to trump our responsibility to stand for the truth or oppose evil in our time. The important thing is for Christians to continue trumpeting the cause of righteousness in this lost world. We must be willing to endure the negative challenges and support what is good. It is better to lose the popularity contest by defending what is right than to forfeit our values and win a contest for which there is no prize.

SHOUT FOR JOY, NOT ATTENTION

LUKE 14:1–14

People like to be noticed. They like to be recognized for a job well done, for a positive contribution, or for achieving a milestone in their lives. It's enjoyable to be singled out for positive accomplishments. Indeed it's important to reward outstanding performance both as a way of saying "Thank you!" and to encourage continued positive traits.

God is fully on board with supporting excellence. Many of the parables and sermons of Christ were focused upon pointing out wisdom, achievement, and tenacity. Moreover, when we Christians stand before the Lord, we are going to be evaluated for our Christ-centered accomplishments in this life. We are promised a life in glory and a crown reflecting the activities of our lifetime.

It's interesting then that the same Lord who intends to shower us with blessings and accolades for the achievements of this life is so intent about how we present ourselves while we're here. There is a difference between recognition we receive at the hand of our Father who loves us and self-recognition all too common in the world today. We must recognize that the Lord wants us to have self-respect and a good healthy self-image. After all, He created us in His image. However, we are not to confuse a healthy perspective about who we are with a conceited, self-serving, narcissistic mindset.

When Jesus criticized the Pharisees, Sadducees, and other church leaders of His day, one of the primary objections He had related to their overpowering self-centered attitudes. They had completely lost their perspective about the intended purpose of their positions. Instead of reaching out to their generation with the love and compassion of their heavenly Father, they had become completely absorbed with their personal hold on power and desire to appear holier and more important than the common person on the street. The result was the priesthood no longer served as a foundational focal point to introduce people to God; rather a perverse exclusionary society of overbearing autocrats emerged.

God never meant for people to lose touch with Him. It was a tragic by-product of the fall. Pride led to the fall, and pride separates us to this day. Christ came as a servant—humble, meek, and compassionate. He didn't seek self-recognition, but only to honor and glorify the Father.

Christ taught us to glorify the Father, not ourselves. He wanted us to understand that self-aggrandizement and conceit are ultimately destructive and despicable. In other words, He wants us to leave the accolades and recognition that may come our way in the hands of our Father who evaluates with love, fairness, and complete honesty.

DOES APOLOGETICS MEAN BEING SORRY ALL THE TIME?

ROMANS 1

It is becoming increasingly unpopular, if not almost unacceptable, to be a Christian. In the media and everyday life, the Christian faith is met with derision and ridicule. No longer is it considered advisable or appropriate to profess a faith in God. In fact, it is difficult to begin a discussion of the salvation offered by Christ in most secular settings. Moreover, discussing faith in Jesus is becoming unacceptable in our public schools, where prayer has been almost completely outlawed.

What is it about our society, not to mention the world, that takes offense at the mere mention of Jesus' name? Why do people question the truth of the gospel? Why is it easier to try to construct a world absent the creative power or overwhelming love of God? So much of our society today is centered on avoiding any acknowledgment of God. It is difficult to incorporate His influence on our daily lives. The unfortunate result of this problem is a generation of people with no understanding of the beauty and value of having a right relationship with the one who created them. People end up wandering aimlessly through life, attempting to gain meaning through a variety of activities and endeavors that, at best, give only a temporary respite from the emptiness of a life excluding God.

It's not reasonable to apologize for our faith. The weight and depth of the gospel add a dimension to earthly existence that far exceeds any alternative offered by the world. The Christian faith recognizes not only the existence and power of God, but it also provides purpose and hope to the believer that transcends this life and points to eternity.

Christ is our Savior. He is our Lord. He loves us enough to sacrifice His own life in order to redeem us to Himself for all time. Importantly He doesn't insist we believe; nor does He present us an ultimatum. Rather He gently offers us the truth in a way that allows us to make our own choice.

It's extremely simple, yet many reject His offer out of hand for reasons vastly more complicated than the choice itself.

There is not sufficient time or space here to ferret through all of the ins and outs of every religion in the world; nor is it my intent to launch a theological discussion of all of the pros and cons of the faith. Numerous volumes have been written by scholars defending the truth of the gospel far exceeding the scope of the instant discussion.

Suffice it to say, in my experience, there is no other faith that honors life, the rights and dignity of others, hope, patience, and love in a more balanced way than Christianity. In no other faith are the rights of the individual not only preserved but emphasized. Moreover, only through Christianity are we taught to love and forgive our enemies, love our neighbor as ourselves, and love the One who loves us the most, our Father in heaven.

Faith in Christ is a choice. The balance that faith offers is a blessing. The available hope transcends the situations we endure, and the joy we receive is impossible to explain. The question is: will you make the decision, or will you languish where you are? It's up to you, and no apologies are accepted.

IF THERE ARE WHITE LIES, DO THEY COME IN OTHER COLORS TOO?

JEREMIAH 9:1–11

How many people do you know whom you can trust? I'm not talking about strictly simple things, but in the deep issues that reach directly into the core of your being? How many people do you know who would tell you the truth, even if it hurt, and still love you afterward? How many people do you know who will answer a question truthfully even if it costs them something, particularly if that something is precious to them?

My bet is, if your experience is similar to my own, the list is rather short. It's difficult to find people who have impeccable integrity in every situation. Indeed it's a challenge at times to get an honest answer to simple questions like "How do I look?" or "Do you think I'm too fat?" All of us ask questions like these and hope to get a positive or constructive response. The problem is that with certain people, we don't always know for sure. What happens when the questions are weightier, when there is more than a potentially wounded ego riding on the response?

Read the morning paper, and you wonder how much is truth versus information colored by the bias or political agenda of the writer or editor of the paper itself. What about the people who themselves are the subjects of the stories? How many of the politicians who claim to fight for our best interests are actually fighting exclusively for their own? How many can you trust?

At every level of our lives, we are confronted with integrity, or the lack thereof. So the question becomes a personal one for each of us to consider and address. Will we be stalwarts of integrity, or will we follow the crowd and simply tell people what they want to hear?

God loves us, but He also loves honesty and holiness. Jeremiah 9:7–9 illustrates the heart of God as He refines and tests His people. Deceits and treachery are not attributes God is willing to accept in His people. He desires that we become examples of integrity in this lost world. God is not willing to bless His people when they cannot be trusted, becoming threats even to themselves.

Honesty is not necessarily an easy thing to achieve. It is a virtue with a price. You may get passed over for a promotion because an honest opinion about your boss's favorite project is not necessarily supportive. You may risk a friendship because you won't hide a misdeed. Regardless of the situation, every question you face will contain an element of integrity. Many times it will be relatively simple to respond appropriately. Sometimes the situation will be quite different. It is those times you will have to decide what you will do, that is, how you will respond.

Jesus said, "I am the way, the truth, and the life" (John 14:6 KJV). He told the truth even when it was not the message people wanted to hear. Indeed, when the truth cost Him His life, He embraced it and never wavered. You may never face a situation where an honest response could cost you your life, but if that moment comes, I would encourage you to embrace the truth. The truth was sufficient for Christ; it ought to be enough for us as well.

WE LOVE HOLDING PEOPLE TO ACCOUNT UNTIL WE BECOME THE HELD

MATTHEW 23

I t's easy, and we learn it at an early age. It's a technique used to gain influence and prestige, not to mention the upper hand necessary to seize power. We practice it throughout our lives and hone the skill to deftly apply it whenever it can yield an advantage. Rarely will we admit that we have the ability or talent to wield such a force, but it's there in all of us waiting for the next opportunity to turn the tide in our favor. It is the finger of blame, and most of us point it without a second thought.

Life teaches us many lessons, and one of the first we learn is the first one to assign fault for a wrong often escapes full scrutiny when the matter becomes known. It's interesting. Most of us learned this skill on the playground with no instruction or preamble. We learned pointing out the faults of others not only focused attention away from ourselves, but also enhanced our position of power and authority. It's a great advantage to be the accuser in any situation because people tend to gravitate more quickly to our position, and we begin to be seen as one who will stand up for what's right and good, even if our motives would belie something more sinister.

In the church, the accusers are often the power brokers. They usually want to be thought of as the keepers of the faith, blameless in most things and easily forgiven in the rest. The accusers look for opportunities to expand their influence, control their environment, and convince others of their deep spiritual understanding. They are often good at quoting scriptures that tend to cut and undermine relationships and can frequently be found at the heart of a controversy. Curiously, but not surprisingly, they consistently react violently when the tables are turned, and they themselves become vulnerable.

Christ was very familiar with the power brokers, those who would rather destroy another than sacrifice their position to save a soul. They permeated the leadership of the temple of His day. It wasn't that God wasn't able to act through His people; it was that the people running the temple left no room for God in their faith.

Simply put, being an accuser is often an indication of the presence of pride. Pride seeks its own gain at the expense of all others. The result is a church that no longer reaches out to the lost. Indeed the lost are convincingly accused and written off. Their lives are lost because the conduit to salvation is cut off by the holier-than-thou attitude of those in control.

Sadly, the truth is that the accused are often guilty, and many recoil and are ashamed. Sadder still, the accusers are just as guilty, often in more contemptible ways than those they blame. The only difference is the one occupying the spotlight. The moral of the story is quite clear: don't be the one who enjoys doing the accounting if you know you couldn't stand up to an audit yourself.

NEITHER GRACE NOR MERCY IS A FOUR-LETTER WORD

PROVERBS 3:21–35

Grace and mercy are not four-lettered words, but all too often we treat them as such. Instead of stepping up to assist with a problem, we turn aside and wait to see what will happen. We find it easy to listen to the story of the Good Samaritan, yet assuming the role of a neighbor often seems foreign and uncomfortable.

Throughout history, there have been people in need, both for reasons of their own making and circumstances beyond their control. Regardless of their situations, however, many of these individuals have gone without assistance or support from those of us with whom they come into contact. Why is that? Why is it so difficult for us to offer assistance when there is a need? Why also is it so difficult for us to stand up for what is right? Why do we rail against the evening news but never get up out of our easy chair to turn the tide?

Unfortunately it is not only in the area of assistance where a problem exists. It is also difficult for many of us to show mercy and grace to the fallen. Christ was able to show mercy to the sinner far more easily than most of the church leaders of His day. He didn't tend to launch attacks upon the fallen from His high horse of self-righteousness and piety. Neither did He compromise away the faith in a self-defeating attempt to be politically correct and tolerant.

Christ stood for what was right and never backed down. When He saw a need, He waded in with both feet, got His hands dirty, and made a difference. He didn't look for opportunities to condemn sinners; neither did He dismiss their shame with a wink. He knew how to deplore what was wrong, stand for what was right, inspire, love, understand, admonish, and encourage all at the same time. He understood the motives of His critics and never backed down from a controversy. Christ understood balance. He knew the difference between right and wrong and acted accordingly.

Would that we could learn from His example and follow it! Would that we could consistently apply the truth of His teaching to our lives without vacillating or misinterpreting the truth! Alas, we are not the perfect person Christ was. We see the world through jaded eyes too easily swayed by cares of the world and sin. Utopia is not here; neither are we its citizens. Nevertheless, we have a mission to fulfill, a calling beyond our shortcomings and faults.

We are called to embody the love of God for this lost world we call home, even if it is only a temporary abode. In that light, it is our duty and responsibility to carry the message of grace and mercy to this world God has given us as a mission field. The call will require dirty hands, tired bodies, passionate persistence, and endless energy. Christ brought all of these elements to His ministry to touch the lives of those He met and to be an example to those of us who would follow Him.

101 REASONS TO LOVE THE LORD: HAVE YOU WRITTEN YOURS YET?

PSALM 30

God forgave me and loves me. Jesus died for me. The Lord has blessed me with a wonderful family and friends. I have a list of blessings, and if I took the time, I could easily come up with at least 101. Indeed, I could easily come up with 1001, although it would take a little while to list them. The trouble is that I don't frequently enough go to the trouble of actually listing my blessings at all.

I will speak for myself, though I don't believe I'm alone. I don't spend enough time thanking God for what He's done for me. In fact, I too often find it easier to ask for more rather than recognize the overwhelming list of benefits I enjoy because of God's love for me. Why is that? Why do I find it easier to ask God for still more when He has already lavished more love upon me than I could ever possibly know?

Not all of this is a self-indictment. God tells us to cast our cares upon Him. It's just that I need to remind myself to say thank-you! It's not a difficult thing, but it is an important thing. God wants to be a significant part of our lives. He wants us to know how much He loves us.

All of us desire to be loved. We want to know we are appreciated for who we are. I believe God is similar in this respect. I think He wants us to love Him because He cherishes being loved. Interestingly, God wants to be loved for the right reasons. He doesn't want a false love based on contrived circumstances. He wants a valid love based upon our individual choice with no inappropriate influence or coercion. That's why we have free will. When we love God freely of our own volition, our feelings are valuable and true. The basis of our relationship will be based on mutual caring and affection.

All of us who know God and love Him understand the depth and breadth of His love for us. When we take time to give it some consideration, we will be overwhelmed by the blessings we have received at His hand. Indeed, when we realize where we would be without God's impact on our lives, it becomes difficult to imagine what we would do.

Many songs have been written and sung, many books have been compiled and read, and many witnesses have spoken and been heard; yet the full sum of the blessings of God is still not known. But we do not need to know the full sum, just the total of what God has done for us. For when we see the mountain of blessings piled at each of our feet, we will be unable to contain our joy.

Go ahead. Make your list. But before you do, it might be a good idea to stock up on paper and a bunch of new pens.

I'VE LEARNED SO MUCH; I KNOW SO LITTLE

PROVERBS 8:1–11

All of life is a learning experience. From the moment we enter the world to the time we leave, we have the potential to gain understanding and wisdom. At first, the learning comes easily. Later as we grow up, learning becomes more difficult. I'm not sure why this happens, but it seems I have to put more effort into learning now than I used to. I've also found I'm more selective about what I am willing to devote time to learn. Obviously, selecting what to learn or not learn is a function of discernment and taste, every bit as much as sheer ability. Nevertheless, learning is an important element of living a fulfilling life.

There is an element to learning, however, that I did not foresee when I was younger but has become more tangible the older I get. It seems to me now the more I learn, the more I realize how little I actually know. It's strange really that I felt I knew so much when I left high school. Looking back, I now realize how blatantly obtuse that notion was.

I really don't think my experience is in any way unique; I've spoken with numerous people who feel the same way. In all honesty, I believe the realization you don't have all of the right answers to all of life's questions is simply a matter of maturity and experience. Additionally, throughout life, you tend to meet people who are more knowledgeable and experienced. You also tend to see an increasingly diverse set of issues that aren't simple cut-and-dried problems. You tend to find the grey areas of life that don't lend themselves to simple or short-term solutions. Finally you also tend to make mistakes, proof positive you don't know enough.

The result of this process, if your attitude doesn't get in the way, usually renders you humbler and wiser. Interestingly, it's the path of experience— both painful and pleasant—that conveys wisdom. As much as it would be nice, experience and its companion, perseverance, cannot be acquired from textbooks. One has to get involved in life to learn from it.

A joy in life is learning. It fulfills a need all of us have to become more than we are, even if we tend to suppress it. I believe God put this desire into each one of us so we could be a blessing to those around us. It is just a little surprising that part of the process would contribute to our humility and help to keep our ego in check. It's wonderful to grasp a new concept yet frightening to know we can never fully grasp the fullness of knowledge possessed by God. In the end, I believe this is a positive thing because it improves our perspective of the absolute greatness of God. Increasing your understanding of God's creation and all of the elements within it improves your knowledge of the Father. Appreciating the infinite magnitude of understanding necessary to hold the universe and our lives together enhances our perspective and awe of God. Ultimately, the more we understand how little we truly understand, the better our ability to worship the only one who does understand.

YOU CAN PROBABLY IDENTIFY THE MOUTH OF THE BODY, BUT CAN YOU NAME THE NAVEL?

1 CORINTHIANS 12:12–31

Some of us approach our place in the church far too casually. Furthermore, we dismiss the importance of others around us who tend to fade into the woodwork. Most of us tend to become complacent about our faith, walk, impact on the body, and concern for others. We let life pass us by, becoming observers of passing events more than instigators of them.

Let me ask you a question: Do you know the names of the people who sat in front of or behind you at church last Sunday? If you know their names, can you remember what they do for a living? Chances are, you don't remember or don't know. That's not too unusual. It's hard to know all of the people in your church, particularly if you attend a large one.

The problem, of course, is that it's hard for us to be involved in our church or get others involved if we don't get to know the people God brings us. Furthermore, if we don't take the time to determine where we can assume a role or recruit another to help us, we will not fulfill God's calling on our lives.

God designed us to be proactive parts of His body here on earth. He is an active God involved in His creation, and He expects us to find a place to make a difference with and for His people. Paul reminds us in this passage that all of us have a role to play. Importantly, each of our roles are unique; each of our roles is vital. That's right. I said vital. There is never an end to the places we can make a difference. The trick is that we may need to be creative about what we do.

That's where you come in personally. You know who you are better than anybody else. You know your abilities and inabilities. Being aware of what you can do sets up the context of where God can use your skills. Now you need to recognize something at this point: God created everyone with a purpose. He also designed a unique spot in the body for you to take an active role. Don't think for a minute that translates to taking a board seat necessarily. Certainly the Lord needs people to fill those roles, but He also needs people passionately involved in hundreds of other activities as well.

As Paul points out in 1 Corinthians, there are a variety of responsibilities to assume, and the Lord needs a variety of people to assume them. In other words, you have a place! Additionally, the people sitting in front of and behind you also have a place to fit in. Maybe you're the one to suggest that or bring it about. Maybe you're the one your church needs to start a new ministry or outreach. Maybe they need a historian or other creative role. Regardless of what it is, you need to find out and jump in. The church does not run itself; the body of Christ runs it. The church grows, but only when people allow themselves to be led by the Holy Spirit to lend a hand and make a difference. Talk to the Lord. Be that next person to jump into the fray. Figure out where the Spirit wants to plug you in, even if it turns out to be the navel!

REVELATION IS A CALL TO ACTION, NOT TO HIDE

REVELATION 22 AND MATTHEW 25:1–13

The last days will be/are very foreboding times. They will be filled with events terrible to behold, not to mention troubling to live through. Christ taught that no one except the Father knows the day and hour of His return. This is significant to us not for the suspense value; rather it is for the incentive it provides for us to get to work expanding the kingdom of God. Too often we look at the end-times prophesies as reasons to withdraw, but I believe Christ intended for us to advance as the adversity of the times becomes greater.

Throughout history, the church has flourished when it was subjected to avarice, scorn, and persecution. Interestingly Christ advised us not only to be prepared for this, but to be ready to overcome it. Moreover, when one considers the parables Christ told about the bride and the servants, it becomes obvious He intended for us to be proactive and involved right up to the moment of His return.

Each day's headlines seem to carry with them some confirmation that biblical prophecy is being fulfilled. Like storm clouds on the horizon, the events of our day herald a change in the climate of our world that has absolutely nothing to do with the weather. Regardless of your position concerning the rapture of the church and other events foretold in Scripture, of one thing we can be certain, that Christ will return and His arrival will sweep across the world like a storm.

The issue we must personally and collectively address as Christians is what we will be doing for the cause of Christ on the day of His return. Suffice it to say, "nothing" is not an acceptable answer. Throughout His ministry, Christ prompted people to action. He did not make excuses for the opposition He encountered, mostly from church leaders. Instead He moved over, around, and through the barriers placed in His way so His message was not lost among the cries of the faithless. The stronger the opposition, the more pointed and assertive was Christ's message.

Christ did not back down from a fight; He stood up to it. He courageously advocated His position directly, without equivocation, and absent of apology. He wasn't rude or discourteous, but He stated His case and backed it up with action.

So where are we? What kind of difference are we making in the world? Where are the changed lives and renewed minds? Are we standing strong for the faith, or are we simply asking the Lord to end the test?

There is much left to do, at least from an earthly perspective. Since we don't know when our Lord will return, we must assume He's leaving us here for a reason. That reason is to reach the world with the gospel. It's our responsibility to continue making a difference even when the world would rather we didn't. Christ wasn't welcomed with open arms by everyone, yet He touched lives and stood the world on its ear. He conquered evil without ever firing a shot or backing down. The clouds are gathering. It's time to gather the harvest before the storm sweeps it away.

IT'S FAR EASIER TO SAY, "IT WON'T WORK" THAN TO FIND A WAY TO MAKE IT HAPPEN

PSALM 121

I can't tell you how many times I've had someone tell me something couldn't be done that I later went out and did. Now I want to be clear. I'm not talking about things that I shouldn't be doing in the first place. With the "shouldn't do" things, I try to remain on the side of what's right. This is also known as staying out of trouble. What I'm talking about here are the new things, the complicated things, the difficult things, the time-consuming things, and the things no one else will attempt; you know, the things you dream of or you aspire to do that take you to a place beyond where you are to where life is better and your experience is expanded.

"It won't work" is one of the most discouraging phrases you will ever hear. It stands in the way of achievement, quells creativity, stifles opportunity, and discourages tenacity. It is a relief that the best course of action is to follow the crowd and take the easy route to achievement. It encourages inaction over risk taking. It is also faithless.

When God created Adam and Eve, one of the things He wanted them to do was discover His creation. He wanted them to augment what He had done and take part in the beauty that surrounded them. Often when we read Genesis, we miss this point. God is creative, and He designed Adam and Eve in His image. He instilled in them a sense of curiosity, intelligence, and creativity to compliment those characteristics within Himself.

We possess the same qualities. I believe the Lord has a plan for each of our lives, a plan that includes reaching beyond who we are at this moment to what we could be in the next. Life is a series of opportunities. It is our job to recognize and seize those opportunities and utilize them to bless the Lord and become all we can be.

One of the problems we often face as adults is losing the ability to dream. Very often we've suffered setbacks in our lives that impact how we move forward. Too often we quell our desire to achieve great things because we remember the pain of past failures. When we allow ourselves to do this, we cheat ourselves out of the greatest possibilities the Lord offers us. History is replete with stories of people who persevered in the face of failure only to achieve a tremendous victory. Often throughout the process of working toward their dream they had to swim against a tide of naysayers who consistently reminded them, "It couldn't be done."

I am sure my experience is similar to yours because I have known setbacks and failures. However, along the way, I've learned God is faithful. I've also learned to submit my dreams to Him and allow Him to direct and support me through the process. When I do this, much of the pressure falls away, and I am able to look out and see the possibilities.

I don't know the future, and I'm sure some of my dreams and ideas will go unfulfilled in my lifetime. I also believe, however, that the Lord influences my dreams and that I can achieve much beyond what I've done to this point in my life. God has a lot in store for me for the rest of my life, and I believe He intends for me to achieve much in the time I remain here. I also believe He has a lot in store for you as well.

IS THE BEST QUESTION, "HOW MANY ANGELS CAN SIT ON THE HEAD OF A PIN," OR IS IT BETTER TO ASK, "WHY WOULD THEY WANT TO?"

PROVERBS 1:1–7

So what's the point really? We argue. We debate. We disagree, but not always amicably. We get into discussions about issues that don't necessarily matter in the overall scheme of things, only to become angry and stop talking at all. We debate important issues such as what people should wear to Sunday services, how loud the music should be, and whether it is all right to go out for lunch after church because it makes somebody have to work.

Throughout the ages, there have been debates within the church. Some of the issues have been weighty, focusing on important ideological issues. Other times the concerns have been frivolous with no eternal implications. Yet the battles raged on. People ranted and raved at one another attempting to prove their point and come out on top.

The result of all of the fighting, in my view, is often negative and divisive. Now instead of one universal church as existed in Paul's day, we have a highly fractured collection of denominations, which are minimally cooperative and frequently antagonistic. What's more, we find it difficult to agree with one another on very many issues and are quick to abandon discourse in the name of seeking a pure faith devoid of human error.

Now I am not naïve enough to think there aren't good reasons to debate scripture to get to the heart of God's intent. I know it's important to know the truth of the Word as it applies to our daily lives and how we approach our faith. However, I know some people have throughout history attempted to put their own personal spin on God's Word to advance some personal agenda. I realize there is a place for debate. I guess my question is: where did we go wrong?

Paul taught unity in the body of Christ. I believe it's safe to say he opposed factions and misleading teaching. Additionally, Paul promoted love between the brethren. Somewhere over the past two thousand years, give or take, we took an erroneous course, which led us to the disjointed body of Christ we live with today. I understand the reasons for many of the changes that have come about, some positive and others negative, but I'm not sure the present situation is the best arrangement. I've grown up with the current situation, as have you. However, at times I wonder how the Lord feels about the whole thing.

Suffice it to say, the current situation is temporary, and for that I'm glad. I know when Christ returns, denominations and disagreements will become a thing of the past, a relic of the former fallen world. It's what we do now, however, that concerns me. Paul instructed us in Romans 12:18 to live peaceably with people, if at all possible. I fully believe this applies to those of us in the church in an even stricter sense.

As long as we inhabit this world, there will be disagreements between us about how to rightly divide Scripture. That's all right. I would even argue healthy. Within that context, however, we need to look for common ground with our brothers and sisters in Christ. We serve one Lord. We have one Savior. He is our Lord, and we are His body, a single unit made up of many diverse parts. Whenever we can, we need to get along with the other parts and keep the debates to a necessary minimum. Besides, I doubt very many angels are worrying about pin sitting, let alone attempting to do it.

WE'RE MORE AFRAID OF OUR QUESTIONS THAN GOD IS

PSALM 88

I was always taught you don't question God. No matter what happened, you were to move on, accepting what came without complaint or query. Experience and study have taught me that it really doesn't quite work that way. I've come to believe God doesn't expect us not to question or try to understand. I don't believe He wants us to be lemmings who don't think for themselves, following the random course of events confronting our daily lives.

When God created Adam and Eve, He wanted to develop individuals who could think and create on their own. He even went so far as to give them free will, choosing what they would do with their lives within the garden He designed. God gave them work to do to challenge their minds so they could grow in wisdom and share their experiences with Him. God even gave them the ability and opportunity to reject Him by eating the forbidden fruit, which tragically they did.

Since the fall, life has been difficult and conflicted. Sin has deprived us of understanding and peace. Life is full of questions and conflicts, while the enemy confronts us at every turn. When we accept Christ as our Savior, we gain hope, but it doesn't end the turmoil and trials. On the contrary, our conflicts, both internal and external, often increase. As a result, we begin to question. We wonder about the depth of our faith, the fairness of events, and even the love of God.

Psalm 88 describes the desperation and longing most of us feel from time to time, but that we usually try to brush over and ignore. We develop the notion that since God is sovereign—and He is indeed sovereign—it is inappropriate to question the events of our lives and His influence on them. The Psalms teach us something different.

If you read through the Psalms, you confront the spectrum of human emotions and experiences. While there are a wealth of praise and worship songs, they alone account for only a portion of the whole. Looking further, you will find a broad collection of what some might consider negative and even distressing thoughts. In short, you will see an array of human emotions from mountaintop highs to valleys of death and despair.

What I find most intriguing about this is that the Bible actually includes both the positive and negative. God didn't filter out the bad in favor of the good. He didn't shun the questions; neither did He condemn the questioner. Why do you suppose this is true? I believe there are several reasons. First, I believe God loves us and wants to know what's going on in our hearts. Second, I believe God wants to meet our needs and wants us to know He will find us wherever we go. Third, I believe God wants us to understand that life is not a bowl of cherries and that others have suffered just as we sometimes do.

Life is full of questions. Sometimes God responds to those questions in ways we can understand; often He does not. Regardless of the reply, we need to know we can be direct with God and that He hears and understands. Our questions are not a problem as long as we're willing to listen to the answer.

DID YOU EVER NOTICE THAT WHILE CHRIST DIDN'T HAVE ANY HANG-UPS, MOST OF HIS FOLLOWERS DO?

2 SAMUEL 12:1–25 AND ISAIAH 53

Christians are not perfect. In fact, it is not an exaggeration to say most of them lead fault-filled lives. Most of the Christians I know confront temptation constantly with considerable failures to their credit as a result. Most can point to times in their lives when they found themselves far from the Lord, off on a tangent that would prove to be very destructive. Most Christians strive for holiness but fall far short of their goal.

Christ was different. He was God incarnate, born into a lost world to bring the Word of Truth and salvation to all of us. He lived a perfect life, never falling to sin. He was a true example to us all, a model for us to follow. Yet there was something very interesting about the company He kept; every last one of them was a sinner, some in very notable ways.

Given Christ's perfection, you would think He would have been more careful about how He picked His friends. After all, a perfect reputation is hard to establish, let alone maintain. However, Christ's focus was not on blamelessness; it was on need. He didn't enter the world after it changed for the better; He came to usher in the change.

Throughout history, God has been executing His plan for redeeming mankind to Himself. From the fall of Adam and Eve forward, the Lord has relentlessly and continually advanced to the place and time where He could be reunited with His creation. The plan is progressing on schedule, and the moment is drawing near when it will be complete. In the meantime, what can we know about Christ and His actions while He was here?

Christ knew every person He would meet would be in need. The world was and is subject to the curse of sin. Given that situation, for Christ to avoid sinful people would have required Him to become a hermit and eliminate all contact with human beings. If He had done that, it would have negated the whole point of His mission here. Christ could not have touched this world with the truth without touching the people who needed to hear it.

Significantly for us, Christ's approach is still valid today. We need to get involved with people who need to hear the truth. We need to understand that the lost have hang-ups and they often don't look or act the way we might like. The big mistake we cannot afford to make is to object to minister to the lost in the first place. Christ was criticized for eating with Publicans and sinners; so should we. Christ brought the truth without being accusatory; so should we. Christ loved without condition; so should we. Christ gave His life for the salvation of many; so should we.

All of us have hang-ups, yet Christ loves us. So should we love others who have hang-ups? If Christ is truly our example, then the answer is quite obviously yes! Don't look to create the perfect world. It is not within our abilities. Rather work to gain followers of Christ in this fallen world where we presently reside. It is up to Christ through the Holy Spirit to take care of the rest. I assure you, He is well up to the task!

WE'RE TOLD TO LOVE ONE ANOTHER, BUT MOST OF US ARE TOO TERRIFIED TO TRY IT

1 PETER 1:13–25

In Christ, we have been changed. We have a renewed spirit and enjoy a right relationship with the Father. The Bible tells us we are new creatures, having the ability to be holy, serve the Lord, and love one another. The question is: how much change do we allow the Lord to bring about? How much of our old nature do we discard, and how fully do we embrace the new person? More pointedly, how much are we willing to let down our defenses and truly love one another?

We're used to hearing how we should love each other in Christ. We quote the second great commandment explained by Christ that we should love our neighbor as ourselves. The words come easily, almost to the point of being cliché. The question is: how many of us truly take the issue to heart? How much do we actually love our neighbor? How much love is enough?

In 1 Peter 1:22, we receive some insight regarding how far we should take our love for others: deeply. Our love is not to be shallow, casual, or limited. We are not supposed to stop short of absolute love, and we are to seek to give our lives for our brothers and sisters in Christ. Unfortunately, we live in a world where things are easily corrupted and the risks are high.

How many of us long to be loved for who we are, with no risk of falling at the hands of our sinful nature? How many of us know how to love deeply without risking crossing the line of impropriety, exposing ourselves to problems we would just assume not encounter? Remember, we are all supposed to love each other. Unfortunately, because sin is so prevalent in this world, not to mention in our hearts, there are practical limits we must observe. It is easy to stumble on the road of good intentions, but good intentions are grossly insufficient anyway.

Sadly, when Adam and Eve fell in the garden, they lost more than their innocence. They lost the opportunity to truly love and enjoy each other and the Lord. No longer could they know the full depth of companionship and devotion God designed them for. They forfeited the unity and compassion God designed into their relationship, finding instead true loneliness for the first time. Their loneliness extends through the ages to us today. We know we are to love each other, offering companionship and fulfillment to our brothers and sisters in Christ, but we stop short of doing so with depth and commitment. Certainly we share affection, but few dare to advance to the level of commitment and passion or, most importantly, sacrifice. Christ's love for us was and is sacrificial. When Christ extended his hand in friendship, a nail was pounded through it. When our love for others moves to the level of sacrifice, we are, at that point, loving along the lines of Christ's example to us all.

Depth of love is important. God notes His first disappointment with the Church at Ephesus is not some deeply theological flaw; rather it was simply a lack of passionate and sacrificial love. God designed passion, and He loves sacrificially. We dream about passion but rarely sustain it in our relationships. Indeed many of us find it difficult to express passion in our relationship with the Lord, even though that's precisely what He desires.

To love deeply is to love sacrificially. It's pouring oneself out for the benefit of another regardless of the cost. We can learn and practice this kind of love in the church. It's the kind of love God wants and the kind of love we all need.

IS IT SIMPLER TO DO THE RIGHT THING OR MAKE AN EXCUSE?

PROVERBS 11:1–13

I bumped it into the wall, and there was a dent. It wasn't a particularly large dent, but it was there just the same. I was tempted to just ignore it and pretend I didn't know anything about it, but I knew in my heart that was probably ill advised. Besides, I was told when I started that if I ever damaged anything and didn't report it, I would lose my job. In effect, it was better to risk retribution at my own hand than to take a chance on someone else pointing the finger. There was also the safety risk that I couldn't afford to take.

The walk to the office was one of the longest I ever took. The speech I gave about how I dented my boss's airplane would prove to be one of the more difficult I would ever make. That's right. I said "airplane." The experience would have been much less traumatic had I dented his Cadillac, but no, it was an airplane, one of several he owned.

It's amazing how certain experiences stay with you for the rest of your life. It doesn't seem to matter how many years pass, you look back and wonder what life might have been like had you never had the bad luck to be involved in the regrettable events of your past. Alas, life just isn't that way. We make mistakes, fall victim to accidents, and come up on the short end of regrettable circumstances. Some of these situations are beyond our control, so they tend to be more easily processed by our conscience. It's the ones that are irrefutably laid at our feet that are more difficult to overcome.

It's tempting to look for an easy way out when you are the perpetrator of a wrong. Dodging blame carries the convenience of not having to be responsible for your actions. The problem is that someone still gets hurt and the blame still rests with you, even if no one else knows.

The Bible teaches us to be upright in our dealings with others. Proverbs 11:5 says, "The righteousness of the upright shall deliver them:

but transgressors shall be taken in their own naughtiness." On its face, this sounds easy and admirable, but in practice, it can be complicated and risky. People don't always admire you when you admit to your failings, even though the Lord knows your heart. The world, and too often other Christians, likes to pile on and add to your embarrassment and shame when your misdeeds and missteps find you out. Hence, that is why it's so difficult to do the right thing. It doesn't always pay off like it did for George Washington and his cherry tree.

Good can come out of bad situations, and it is worth it to do the right thing even when the immediate outcome is unpleasant or painful. At very least, you get to have a clearer conscience and get to know you did what the Lord would have you do. Additionally people will know you can be trusted, even when the chips are down. Finally you learn God is faithful despite your shortcomings and failures. I turned myself in, got lectured, learned a lesson, and kept my job. I never had to apologize for lying and gained a little integrity through the process.

Through it all, I learned that God is good and His teachings are true.

IN THE FINAL ANALYSIS, THE BEST TITLE YOU CAN HOLD IS "CHILD OF GOD"

JOHN 1:1–14

Position, title, and status; most of us compete for these every day, whether we realize it or not. We go to school to get an education so we can gain a professional title describing our academic achievements. We get jobs in the marketplace complete with admirable titles communicating to the world our career progress. We join social organizations and assume various leadership roles with titles reflecting our value to the organization. Even having children elevates us to the positions of Mom or Dad.

Regardless of our place in life, we will always carry titles describing our relationships with others and positions of authority and responsibility. We will always be identified based upon our achievements, attitudes, ideas, and personalities. People will rank us based upon how easy or difficult we are to work with and will want to associate with us (or not) based upon their perceptions of who we are. In short, our identities are all multifaceted and complex. We all wear many hats through the course of our lives with varying degrees of influence in each.

From this context, we all have to decide which of the positions we hold are the most important. Which positions most aptly describe who we really are or would most like to be? In other words, what are your true priorities in life? What were you designed for, and where is the Lord taking you? Are you letting the Lord guide you to the place where you belong? When you complete your stint in this life, what is it about your life that will matter for eternity?

Life changes and priorities shift, but the Lord is constant. Accordingly, we can be sure He is interested in the outcome of His investment in each of our lives. Moreover, we can be certain He wants us to progress through this life to a closer walk with Him. We need to realize we will wear many hats as we grow and mature in Him. Some of the positions we may occupy will cast us as an apprentice while others will present us as the teacher. Regardless of the place we currently stand, Christ always has a plan for us to fulfill. We need to gain the wisdom to recognize that our Lord is continually trying to enhance who we are to become all He designed us to be.

As we move through this life, we need to remember the titles we hold at any given time are only temporary. Regardless of the apparent authority and power we may wield, it's only a momentary occurrence. Time passes, authority changes, and others step into the positions we once held. Positions we once viewed as permanent prove to be all too fleeting, quickly passing into the short piece of history we call life.

There is, however, one title we can hold dear that does matter for more than just a few short years. It's a title affording more honor, joy, fulfillment, and hope than any other. It has a noble name, though many of us don't think of it as such very often. It's a name conferred with little preamble, at no cost, and to everyone who will accept it. It's available to you, and it will matter for all eternity. It's a simple name. You may have heard of it. It's "Child of God," and you can obtain it today. All you have to do is ask.

I DON'T LONG FOR
CHRIST ENOUGH

PSALM 25

I live with this person who likes to push my buttons! He claims to love the Lord, but his efforts to draw closer consistently come up short. He shows up for church on Sunday but tends to forget he was even there by the end of the day. To say he is inconsistent would be an understatement, and his desire for the Lord tends to wane all too easily. He's a likable person, or at least he tries to be, but he all too often finds ways to disappoint those he cares about the most. I wish I could tell you it was someone else, but it's not. It's me.

Plain and simple, I am a sinner. I've been this way from birth, and I've concluded I will probably be this way for some time to come. It's easy to become discouraged about it, and at times I find the disappointment overwhelming. I understand Paul's complaints about being stuck in a sinful body. It's easy to sin, and I don't even have to practice to do it well.

But there's another side to the story. It gives me hope and encouragement despite the difficulties I've faced and the mistakes I've made. Christ has given me grace. It was a gift. It covered my sins and washed them away. Because of Christ's sacrifice on the cross, I have life, forgiveness, and love. I could never deserve these things on my own, even though I wish I could. God designed me to love and serve Him. My life is not a mistake, even though I own a collection of them.

I used to think I had to attain a certain level of holiness before I could do much of anything for the Lord. Later I decided that if I waited until I was holy, I'd never do anything in this life. Not one to sit still, I decided to start trying to live for the Lord day by day and work on His behalf despite and through all of my shortcomings.

Moving forward has been a slow process. I still trip, fall, get bruised, run off the road, and miss the mark on an all too consistent basis, but I'm giving more and more of my life to the Lord every day. It's not an easy process, but I'm reaping more joy from it all the time. Working and living for the Lord are the most rewarding things I've ever done. Each day I move into the process I become happier and more fulfilled.

Christ is becoming the focus of my life. The process is by far long from being complete, but I am on my way. As I move forward, I realize more and more how far I was from where I'm supposed to be and how far I still have to go, but there is motion. I'm no longer waiting for holiness to simply drop down on me, I am trying to take steps toward it. God has called us to be holy because He is holy, so I'm endeavoring to comply.

Through it all, I've learned the key to focus on is loving Christ. Instead of living the do/don't list, I've simply started to try to love Jesus more. I'm more motivated by my relationship with Him than a set of rules. I have a desire for Christ in my heart, and even though I don't long for Him enough, I long for Him more than I did before. Tomorrow I'll long for Him more still. Finally, someday I'll see Him face-to-face, the longing will stop, and I will be fulfilled.

I TEACH SUNDAY SCHOOL, SO I SHOULD BE EXEMPT FROM TEMPTATION

1 CORINTHIANS 10:1–13

It's just not fair! I've committed my life to Christ, been a church member for as long as I can remember, and taught Sunday school for about twenty years. I've tried to walk the walk and talk the talk, just like Christians are supposed to do. I even went to a Christian university because I wanted an appropriate spiritual dimension to my education. You'd think with all of the Christian emphasis I have tried to have in my life that I would no longer be tempted by sin and the things of the world. But guess what? It just isn't so.

Sin is an infection, a disease handed down to each one of us compliments of Adam and Eve. I can't say I necessarily blame them. I would probably have done the same thing had I been in their place. The sad thing for me is just that I wish sin hadn't come onto the scene in the first place. Unfortunately that is not the world as we know it, and it won't be until Christ returns. So what do we do in the meantime?

Pray! Pray for ourselves, for one another, without ceasing. The Bible instructs us to do this, but most of us don't. It's just not something many of us have incorporated into our day or perspective. I'm learning on this journey through my life that prayer and, more specifically, my relationship with Christ is the source of my strength and hope. The sins in my life are the barriers that prevent me from drawing closer to Christ and the Father. Their existence closes doors and erects barriers, preventing me from drawing close to the Savior I love. In the end, I become frustrated and angry, usually with myself, for not being the person I was designed to be. I try to do the right things but tend to find myself where I don't want to be.

Why do I bring any of this up? Simple! I want to encourage you to keep working out your salvation. Put your best efforts into letting go of the sins that beset you and strive to move closer to the Lord. In addition to that, I would ask you to pointedly pray for those you know in leadership positions in your church. They are trying to advance the truth and mission of God in a particularly hostile environment. The more effective they are, the more likely the enemy is coming against them aggressively and relentlessly. Understand that these folks are probably trying to do the right thing, but they very likely face considerable obstacles in their walk and ministry.

How do I know this? Simple really! It's happening to me! My experience has been that the more I try to do in my life for the Lord, the more the enemy comes against me. The relationship of temptations to activity for the Lord in my life seems to be directly proportional.

In the end, I would note that Jesus loves you and me. His Holy Spirit is here to help us, and His love and guidance apply to each one of us. Moreover, Christ loves us personally and intimately. This means you every bit as much as it means me. Focus on the love of Christ for you personally. Emphasize your relationship with Him. It's in the relationship and love that you will find the power and desire not to sin. Look for it! Christ is waiting!

THE HARDEST MESSAGES TO BRING ARE THE ONES THAT APPLY TO YOURSELF

PSALM 6

There have been numerous times when I've listened to a message at church or read a biblical passage and the words seemed to jump out and grab me. The Holy Spirit moves in my heart particularly at those times to convict me about sins and shortcomings, provide encouragement at a particularly distressing time, or inspire me to move into a new area of growth. During those times, I experience a closer relationship with the Lord and feel prompted to make the changes a growing relationship requires.

The Holy Spirit loves us and responds to us individually and intimately. His passion for us and the direction of our lives transcends our understanding. He is a close personal friend who is both creative and persistent in his pursuit of our hearts. He desires to give us the opportunity to gain a more intimate relationship with the Father through Jesus Christ.

Oftentimes we get caught up in our daily activities and forget to pursue the relationship we need the most. Instead we wander off and do our own thing. In the name of finding ourselves, we get lost or embrace more of the world and less of Christ.

I am a Sunday school teacher. I've been one for going on twenty years. During that time, I've had numerous experiences when I felt the lesson I was preparing was exclusively for me. I'm sure the Holy Spirit touched the heart of others on many of those occasions, but I often felt like He just had me in mind. I'd like to tell you most of those occasions were inspiring and uplifting, but that would be a lie. Many of the times the Lord was convicting me of sin or prompting me to grow up spiritually.

It's my understanding that I'm not unique in this experience. Many other teachers, preachers, and Christian authors I've heard or read about have had similar experiences. With all of them, it's the same; the Holy Spirit prompting growth, repentance, or redirection. Thankfully the Holy Spirit has been gentle and kind in His influence. He has continually loved and nurtured me toward a closer relationship with the Father and Jesus Christ. The hardest part has been admitting to myself the message was for me. I've learned to listen to the prompting of the Holy Spirit even when he chooses to do so via the words that are coming out of my own mouth.

IT'S WHAT'S ON THE INSIDE
THAT COUNTS, AND THAT'S
THE SCARY PART!

MATTHEW 15:1–20

How well do people know you? How open is your heart? If everything inside your heart were laid out for the world to see, how would you feel? For most of us, these are disturbing questions we would just as soon not even answer. For most of us, the truth is we are two people: the person we let the world see and the person we hope they never meet.

None of us is perfect, yet all of us want to be. We want to be the best athlete, the best businessperson, the best performer … the list goes on. Unfortunately, all of us fall short of the mark most of the time. Even if we do succeed and accomplish something notable, the recognition is short-lived, and we soon descend back into mediocrity.

The issue here, however, goes far beyond the external performance recognized and criticized by the world. Rather we need to focus on the defining character issues that shape our perspective and approach to life. What is it about who we are that will impact how we respond in various situations? Will we be the person who loves no matter the cost, or will we be the one who seeks to maneuver into positions of advantage at every turn?

Our response to the situations arising in life depends entirely upon how we view ourselves as influenced by who we really are deep down inside. We may respond to an opportunity based on how we think others perceive us, or we may react based on who we really are. The sad part is that there is a difference between the two. Too often, we would like to respond in a certain way, but we change our approach based upon who is in the room.

The question, "Who's watching?" is a very relevant one. We will respond to others differently in different situations. Sometimes a varied response is necessary and even positive. A problem arises, however, when our motives are less than admirable and we have a hidden agenda. Christ criticized the Pharisees in this passage not because following the law and cleanliness were not important, but because their motives for following the rules were perverted. The Pharisees were not worried about personal hygiene or the health of their parishioners. They were concerned about appearing more holy than anyone else and asserting their authority and position. Who the Pharisees were versus who they were supposed to be were two very different things. Furthermore, the truth about who they were on the inside was something far afield from whom they purported to be.

So who are we? Speaking for myself, I'm someone other than who I would like to be. I struggle with my sinful nature constantly and all too often lose the fight. The issue, though, is to continue the battle! None of us will be perfect in this life, but that doesn't mean we shouldn't try to achieve something better. The important thing is to recognize and address the spiritual conflict going on within you. Christ, through the Holy Spirit, can help you make a difference. You will never achieve perfection while you're here, but you can begin the process of becoming more like the Savior who called you.

IF THE BIBLE ISN'T THE INFALLIBLE, INSPIRED WORD OF GOD, WHY BOTHER?

2 TIMOTHY 3

Many would argue today that at best, the Bible is a collection of nice ideas and some good stories, but not much else. Others would say the Bible contains numerous inaccuracies and is totally out of date for today's society. A significant number do not believe the Bible is the infallible, inspired word of God. These ideas are disturbing in and of themselves. To think a large portion of this planet's population rejects the veracity of the Bible is at best worrisome. To understand a fair number of churchgoing people who consider themselves Christians subscribe to the above-noted positions is disastrous.

Paul, in his second letter to Timothy, gives some insight into what we are experiencing in our world today. His warning to Timothy is as timely now as it was on the day it was penned. We are part of a world careening into the final days. The evidence is all around us and continually updated and captioned in the evening news. We can see the beginning of the end, and it would serve us well to recognize it.

That people choose not to believe the Scriptures is not a new issue. It's as old as the Bible itself. The problem here is that many claim to have faith but then fail to follow through on fully believing the Word. Their reasons for not believing are numerous and far-reaching. Sadly, they think they are being better Christians for disavowing portions of the Bible that make them feel uncomfortable or that they do not understand. They also readily dismiss components of Scripture that do not play to their political or social sensitivities.

When it comes to the Scriptures, compromise is not an acceptable alternative. The Bible is not a book that can be divided into detachable segments so the reader can selectively choose to believe only those sections that fit popular opinion. The Bible is a book that must be studied and understood in its entirety. To select only those portions that fit the reader's understanding or sensitivities is both destructive and contradictory.

The Bible claims to be the infallible Word of God. It's an all-or-nothing proposition. Either the Bible is a reliable source of information helping us to understand who God is and our relationship to Him, or it isn't. There is no middle ground. We must decide to believe the Bible's claims or not. We cannot, however, have it both ways. We cannot attempt to pacify some internal desire to believe in something only to reject considerable portions of the content to satisfy our personal critique of what we feel it should say. Either the Bible is the inspired Word of God or it isn't. There is no middle ground.

In short, we need to have the courage as Christians to stand up for what is true and right. We need to have the intestinal fortitude to take on the complete message of God and conform our life to it. The Bible does not allow us to attempt to conform God to our image; nor does it provide a place for us to replace or modify His thoughts with our own. Faith in the Word of God is an all-or-nothing choice. The question is: will we have the courage to confront that choice with all of its implications or not, and if we answer yes, what will we do about it?

DON'T CHANGE CHURCHES; LOVE THE ONE YOU'RE IN

EPHESIANS 4:1–16

I love my church. It is not perfect. Its people are flawed. They make mistakes. The services do not always start and end on time. Sometimes I get asked to do something I don't care to do; still other times I do not get asked at all. Occasionally I get an unexpected hug from someone showing me Christ's love, but most often I don't get hugged at all. My church is an unusual place, a place fraught with challenges, both positive and negative. The people there don't have all the answers, and they have some unusual questions. It's one of the few churches where I've felt at home.

I've attended several churches over the years from a variety of backgrounds. In each one, I've found people who love the Lord, people who truly wish to develop a close relationship with the Lord. What's strange, however, is the number of people I have met at all of those churches who do not seem to last too long. They show up one Sunday, and before you know it, they are happily involved and on fire for the ministry. Then something weird happens! They disappear! Occasionally I find out they left to attend another church, and sometimes they leave without a trace.

Now I'm not naïve enough to think something did not cause these people to depart. I just find it strange that a person so dedicated one day can simply be gone the next. To those of us left behind, it can be quite discouraging. Personally I think it is a function of the world in which we live and the level of independence we have deeply ingrained in us.

Obviously we could spend countless pages discussing why people move around from church to church. Numerous articles and books have been written on the topic. It's certainly been the subject of innumerable sermons over the years. No church is immune, and very few people haven't changed churches at some point in their lives. To be candid, on rare occasions for a variety of reasons, I have done it myself.

My concern here is the propensity to change churches frequently with very little concern for commitment and unity. When you consider this passage in Ephesians, it becomes readily apparent that church unity and cohesiveness are not new issues. Even at the beginning of the development of the Christ-centered church, dissension in the ranks was a problem. The striking thing is that many of the reasons for disunity are the same today as they were in Paul's day. People still have the same kinds of problems with pride, sin, and disparate theological positions. Yet the church survives.

But what about us? Where are we going to stand on this issue? Let me suggest a few ideas. First, I understand the requirement to find an evangelical Bible-believing church. If you don't have this, you don't have much of anything. After that, the issues become more personal and fuzzy. Suffice it to say, it is best if you can find a Christ-centered church where you can become one of the family. When you do, join and stay. Remember, relationships are a function of our choices. We have to decide to try to make them work. It doesn't just magically happen. The same is true of a church. To be a part, you have to decide to put forth the effort, and then you have to be committed. Like Paul taught, join the body, seek unity, and love the brethren. In the end, it's up to you!

THE CHURCH OFTEN GETS A BAD RAP IN THIS WORLD; SOMETIMES IT EVEN DESERVES IT!

JAMES 2:1–13

I can't begin to tell you the number of times I've heard stories from people about not being welcomed in the church. They range from the "you're not one of our kind" variety to the "you've committed too grievous a sin" type. These folks have faced attitudes of indifference, disgust, and disdain. They received grief instead of mercy or judgment instead of forgiveness. In short, they've encountered a place contrary to their needs and unwilling to grant them care. For them, the church has not been a safe repose; rather it has been a chamber of horrors.

How is it that mercy fails and love falters where it's supposed to be known best? Why do the people of God fail to communicate the message of love and faithfulness to those who long for their call? When will the message be told to the lost if the church is afraid to visit and even welcome them? Can Christ be served by those who will not recognize need or those who refuse to accept anything but perfection?

Now don't get me wrong. There are many wonderful people attending churches around the world who honestly love the Lord, doing their level best to communicate the gospel of Christ to this lost world. They put their hearts and souls into the Lord's work, often performing countless thankless tasks on His behalf to usher those who will come into the kingdom.

My concern is with those whose focus is more on their position than reaching the lost, those who are more concerned with who's on the board rather than who's at the altar. For some, Christianity is something akin to a large social club. To them, church is attended primarily to be seen by others who might show up or to be thought of in the community as a good person. Instead of listening to the sermon to learn how to move their hearts closer to Christ, they are more concerned with when the preacher will finally quit talking so they can get out the door and be first in line for lunch.

We can't let the church become the victim of our own shortcomings. We have to understand we all have sinned and need the saving grace of Christ our Lord. We must see the need in our own lives for a Savior and translate that into merciful hearts yearning to meet the needs in the lives of others. We are called to judge between right and wrong, thereby standing up for the good. However, we are also called to summon the lost who have yet to learn the truth, those who have never known of righteousness nor understood that they should desire it.

Christ functioned in a world lost in sin, just as we do. He was perfect in all His ways and was not afraid to call sin what it was. He also understood mercy, however, and had a knack for drawing the lost to Himself. Sadly, He was criticized for his efforts by none other than the leaders of the church. Today's church suffers from the presence of the same kind of critics. It is our job as followers of Christ to move beyond their shortsightedness to become pastors like Christ, to love the lost and to share the truth with those who will listen.

I'M A CREATION, NOT
A MUTATION

PSALM 139

I hate the argument that faith and science do not mix. Some would even go so far as to say each contradicts the other. We live in an age of competing theories and philosophies, each vying for not only our attention but our allegiance. I find it amazing how quickly the world at large looks for ways to exclude God from the discussion when it comes to scientific discovery and ever-changing technology.

Science has done well in many respects defining the origin of the universe and life itself. Academics can readily explain the complexities of the workings of our universe down to reasonable conjecture of how and why stars and planets form. Moreover, we have gained greater understanding of biological life and improved our insight into the human genome. Every day scientists study and learn more about how things work. They have gained insight into physical systems to such an extent that they can now logically explain things previously considered miraculous.

The problem is, many who choose not to believe in God have attempted to parlay our improved scientific understanding into prima facie evidence supporting their case. Instead of seeing the wonder, beauty, and order existing in creation as supportive of the notion of God's existence, they attempt to cancel any need for God by explaining Him away as unnecessary baggage.

Ever since the fall of Adam and Eve, the enemy has attempted to widen the gap between God and human beings. If he could do it through superstition, he would. If he could do it through deception, he did. Now he tries to set a case against the Father by using his own creation as apparent evidence against Him.

The universe is now seen in some circles as a self-sustaining and self-defining system. To the extent he can, the enemy has tried to convince people there are irreconcilable conflicts between scientific discovery and biblical teaching. Nothing could be further from the truth. The Bible has consistently proven true when held up against the backdrop of scientific reasoning and investigation. The Bible, when taken in context, lines up very well with known scientific fact. Differences have only arisen when the facts have been misinterpreted or arranged with underlying bias attempting to leave God out of the picture.

The problem for the unfaithful is that the picture keeps pointing back to God. Time and again, new and existing scientific discoveries about the fine-tuning of the universe and the complexity of biological life point increasingly toward the existence of a creator. It is man's misinterpretation of the facts, not the facts themselves, that errantly points people away from God.

The problem is not that faith in God is scientifically unsupportable. The problem is that too many people who would rather not believe in the first place attempt to bend the facts to support their erroneous position.

God is powerful. He has the ability to design and sustain the universe. Moreover, He has the ability not only to create life but also to assemble it into final finished products of His own choosing. God is not limited by human intellectual unwillingness to accept His capabilities; neither is His existence threatened or diminished by humanity's refusal to believe.

WE NEED TO TALK MORE ABOUT THE GOOD KIDS

PSALM 127

I love my kids! I could spend hours telling you how proud I am of them and their accomplishments. They're bright, energetic, involved, and focused. They have a good idea of where they are going with their lives and are taking the necessary steps to achieve their goals. I also love my kids' friends. They have learned to associate with high-caliber people with good characters and positive outlooks. What can I say? I have been blessed with the best.

My children have accomplished a lot, I believe, because of their faith and a heart for the Lord. They set their minds to certain tasks and then set about to successfully achieve them. They have balance in their lives, and it shows up in every aspect of their lives.

My children are wonderful people, but they are not the only good kids out there. In fact, there are large numbers of kids growing up around this country who are achieving success because they too understand what is important. I submit you will find the vast majority of the successful kids have strong parental support at home and excellent teachers at school. I would also submit the most successful kids and their parents have faith in the Lord.

While I can't speak for others' families, I can tell you from my experience, the combination of faith and parental involvement makes a huge difference in kids' outlook on life. My wife has been an educator for over twenty years, and her experience confirms the above observation. Interestingly, parental involvement and faith seem to transcend social status and location. Having taught in both an inner-city and suburban environment, my wife has told me that the best students with the best outlook on life come from homes with supportive parents who have an abiding faith.

As a Christian parent, you have an opportunity to provide your child with a strong foundation upon which to build their life. While there are no guarantees, your kids will have a much-improved opportunity to achieve success in their lives if they learn their life skills from you and adopt your faith in Christ. There is no substitute in life for the positive influence of loving faithful parents on their children. The Bible, in several places, promises us if we train up our children to follow the Lord and do what is right, they will be blessed and be a blessing to others.

When considering my family, I can't think of any greater promise than that of my children being blessed. Life can be very difficult. We can face a variety of problems and challenges that may overwhelm us. Indeed, growing up in today's world is a very different proposition. Kids face problems and issues far more complicated and difficult to manage than past generations. The front page of the newspaper depicts every horror known to man with glaring frequency and blatant graphics.

God gives us children as a blessing. It's up to us to give our children the best shot possible to achieve God's plan for their lives. Don't be afraid to be in love, be involved, and be blessed by your kids. Accentuate their achievements, and correct their mistakes. Lead them into a life with Christ and enjoy the blessings of God's promises fulfilled.

CHRISTIANITY IS NOT SUPPOSED TO BE FASHIONABLE; IT'S SUPPOSED TO BE RIGHT!

MATTHEW 5:13–20

Standing up for what is right - is there anybody left who really knows how to do this? Today it seems we have two extremes in the Christian world. On one hand, we have people who are so into piety and legalism they can't get close enough to an unbeliever to bring up the gospel message of Christ's saving grace. On the other hand, we have people who are so willing to compromise every facet of their faith that you can't tell if they will stand firm for Christ on any substantive issue. Today we tend to want to be on top of the latest politically correct issue rather than stand apart for the veracity of the truth Christ taught. This is a dangerous crossroad for the church, one necessitating a move toward a balanced faith founded on clear biblical teaching.

Interestingly, this is not a new problem. Obviously, Christ encountered the same issue in His day. I suppose this is evidence human nature hasn't changed all that much. We still seek acceptance from the crowd rather than stand apart for something important. Christ did not compromise His faith or message. Importantly, He also never lost the ability to journey into the world of lost people offering an alternative to the destruction of sin. When He spoke He was compassionate, yet firm. He stated the facts about what comprised a life sold out to God without taking on the airs of the church leaders of His day who so easily blew off the truly needy and lost of the world.

Christians today often find it too easy to surrender the moral high ground in order to appear more tolerant of opposing views. Instead of stepping up to support and defend the truth with a loving and balanced message of faith, we tend to back down and seek a middle ground position.

I will be the first to admit that balancing a compassionate message of God's love while firmly standing for the truth is not easy. In fact, it's particularly difficult. Nevertheless, standing up for the reliability of Scripture as a basis for living life and finding God are two of the most important things a Christian can do.

Read the entirety of Matthew 5:13–20. Christ was more than encouraging believers; He was calling them to stand up and stand out as beacons of hope to a lost world. Christ did not say the world would jump up and say "Amen!" In fact, based on the message here, Christ implied the temptation to stand down and compromise would be considerable.

Do not overlook the fact that the call to holiness was not abated with the advent of grace. Indeed Christ called people to holiness throughout His ministry. One change that did occur was that Christ called people to a relationship with Him and He was holy. Therefore, holiness became an opportunity to draw near to God as part of a relationship with Him. No longer was doing what was right an attempt to earn one's way to heaven; now it was an offering of love to the Father of love. So seek to enhance your relationship with God, and stop trying to impress a world that's not paying attention anyway.

FAITH ISN'T BLIND; IT'S FARSIGHTED

HEBREWS 11

So much of life is a question. We don't get to know what tomorrow will bring. We don't have insight into the future. We observe the events of our lives in a real-time series of experiences synchronized with the ticking of the clock, never accelerating, never slowing down. Each moment passes, never again to return. We can anticipate some of the events we hope and plan for, but when they arrive, they evaporate quickly into the past. We cannot hold them in our hand; nor can we recapture the reality.

Every day we live is a gift from God. It is something we can enjoy, but not possess. The moments we have come from a gracious Father who loves us. He designs each experience and ordains every opportunity. In the end, they are His alone, segments of time that wash past us, flowing from future to past in an eternal procession. We experience life in one direction, sometimes with happy anticipation, other times with fear and trepidation.

What, however, if we don't believe? What if we have no basis for faith? Some in this world argue vehemently against the existence and/or influence of the Father in our lives. They support the notion that any faith in God is blind or delusional. Lacking faith themselves, they can offer no supportable reason for our existence. Purpose in life becomes an abstract construct founded simply on their belief in their own existence and abilities. Faith in the possibility of positive outcomes, not to mention hopes and dreams, is simply an arbitrary decision of an individual founded on nothing more than their personal bias toward anticipated life events over which they have little influence or control.

The Bible teaches us life is not arbitrary. Indeed the events of our lives are part of an overall plan designed by a Creator who loves us. We can have faith and hope because God grants it to us. It is merely up to us to decide to accept it or not. It's the acceptance of God's influence in our lives that is left up to us to decide, and decide we must.

Faith in God is effectively synonymous with belief in purpose. Outside of a relationship with a Creator who exists, there is no basis for purpose and no basis for faith. God is the source of our reason for being. Nothing else is transcendent enough to provide any rational basis for hope. Accepting God exists, which in my opinion is the only rational position, creates a basis for having faith. Faith, in its simplest terms, means trusting our Creator to follow through on His plan as it relates to our lives. When we believe God exists, we have reason to believe God acts. If God acts as His Word says, we know He is consistent in His love for us, and we have a foundation for trusting Him.

While it's true we don't always understand why things happen the way they do, it is also true that God is sovereign and trustworthy. We know God acts on our behalf because He tells us so in His Word. The events around us may appear at times to indicate the contrary, but nothing happens outside of God's master plan. We can have faith in God because He is reliable. We can have faith because God has our best interests in mind. We can have faith because God's perspective is eternal. He is playing for the long haul. We can have faith because it represents our foothold on an eternal reality.

TOLKIEN DIDN'T WRITE THE ORIGINAL RETURN OF THE KING

REVELATION 19

My favorite films of all time are *The Fellowship of the Ring*, *The Two Towers*, and *The Return of the King*. Combined, these three films beautifully tell the story of *The Lord of the Rings* written by J. R. R. Tolkien. From what I've read about him, Tolkien did not care for allegory, so reading biblical characters into his story is probably more coincidental than intentional on his part. Nevertheless, the Christian background Tolkien brought to his work obviously influenced his perspective regarding the obvious conflict between good and evil.

It strikes me that *The Lord of the Rings* communicates to us on many levels and resonates hope to us all. It is easy to relate to the characters and their combined struggle to overcome overwhelming adversity. Although strictly fictional, the context of this trilogy translates well into the world situation we currently face and the prophetic return of a King who is anything but fictional. Our King, the Lord of heaven and earth, is coming to assume a throne that has been reserved for Him from the beginning. His kingdom is real and shall have no end. His reign shall be in righteousness, and through Him, the world will know peace. It almost seems too good to be true, but it's something we can all hope for.

But what of our conflicts today? How do we cope with the events surrounding us? Given the evening news, how do we maintain the courage necessary to see things through to the appearance of our King?

Watching world events can be completely disconcerting. It seems every day the world turns more chaotic. There are sensational stories of violence and reminders of man's inhumanity to man constantly crossing our television screens. In the name of tolerance and political correctness, moral values and social standards long considered pillars of our lives are struck down and discarded. In our world, it's morally acceptable to take a life through abortion but detestable to say a prayer in a school. The world insists Christians be tolerant of other religions while Christianity is derided as being out of fashion and ineffective.

We live in a world much like Middle Earth. Dark clouds are rising on the horizon, and hope for the survival of mankind grows increasingly dim. The forces of evil are banding together to march against the last strongholds of peace and hope. If we allow ourselves to get caught in the ever-growing cacophony of hatred and anarchy screaming at us from an overly zealous media machine, we can lose all hope and capacity to cope with a world out of control.

God, however, is in control, and while we can't dismiss the events around us as unimportant or irrelevant, we do not need to approach them with fear. In the end times, we have been told we will face adversity and suffer persecution. We will face trials and tests, but in the end, our King will reign. We can have hope because the return of the King will not be a work of fiction, but a reality that will change the course of history. Our King will occupy a throne that will endure forever. He will be King of Kings and Lord of Lords, and we shall be His people reigning with Him forever.

DO YOU HAVE THE PASSION OF *THE PASSION OF THE CHRIST?*

MARK 15

I t's the Easter season again, and as is becoming my custom, I spent time watching *The Passion of the Christ*. In my opinion, Mel Gibson captured much of the torture and pain our Savior suffered as he took upon Himself the sins of the world, including my own. From this context, the whole story of Christ's death and resurrection overwhelms my ability to understand the kind of love Christ has for each and every one of us. Why would God care so much for us that He would make a provision for us to be redeemed unto Him? Indeed what is so important about human beings that God would allow them to brutally murder His own child just to reestablish a relationship with them? I look at my life and think God came out on the short end of the deal.

There is an even more perplexing issue that also comes to mind. It is an enigma bordering on nonsensical. Christ came into the world to show us God's love. He offers us a free gift of eternal life through His shed blood, yet the world does seemingly everything it can not only just to ignore, but to overtly reject His offer. Think about it for a moment. What is the rational basis of turning down a gift of a joy-filled life spanning all eternity? The gift includes a perfected body that is not corruptible by disease or death. Moreover, the recipients of the gift will never know want or need of any kind.

So if you can, please explain why so many reject the opportunity to enjoy being with a Savior who loves them. Considering the gift is offered for free, it's tragic and astounding all at the same time.

If you are reading this and have never asked Christ into your heart to be your Savior, I would encourage you to do so now. It's really not difficult, and it will change your whole perspective on life and eternity. All you have to do is recognize the sins in your life qualify you as one in need of forgiveness and then ask the Lord Jesus to forgive you and be your Savior. The prayer doesn't have to be long or eloquent, just honest. Indeed, the thief on the cross simply asked Christ to remember him when he came into His kingdom. From that simple request, Christ offered an eternity in paradise, the gift he offers to each and every one of us.

For those of you who have already tasted of the goodness of Christ's joy and salvation, I would simply encourage you to take the time to truly appreciate the gift you possess. It's too easy for Christians to become complacent about their faith and lose the zeal they once had for the gospel of Christ. This world pulls us in hundreds of directions, most of which are away from our Lord. Take the time to contemplate the overwhelming process Christ went through to provide His priceless gift. For the gift is indeed priceless, and it came at an incredible cost.

IF YOU GET IT ALL, WHAT WILL YOU DO WITH IT?

LUKE 12:35–48

It's the American dream to find fortune and prosperity and live life to its fullest. We quote scripture and ask for the Lord's blessings. Often the Lord is gracious and provides for us well beyond our needs. He gives to us abundantly and shows us His favor and love. His kindness is overwhelming as He pours out His love to us. God is our provider, our helper, our friend. He shields us from harm and watches over us. We ask Him, and He often obliges us with the desires of our hearts.

God is good, and He knows how to bless His own. Yet how often do we think about what we are going to do with the blessings we've been given? You see, the responsibility we have as God's servants begins when we receive His blessings. His answer to our prayers is the beginning of the story, not the end. This brings us to a fundamental question: what will you do for the Lord with the blessings you receive?

I really like this passage in Luke because it is about responsibility. Too often we want to overlook our duties as Christians. We want to enjoy what the Lord has given us, but we don't want to think beyond that level. It's important to assess the Lord's blessings and consider why He's given something to us. Nothing in our lives happens outside of God's plan. Everything we experience has the potential to be a blessing either to us and/or to someone else, yes, even the difficult things. If you have been given something special, share it with others. If you have endured a trial and drawn closer to the Lord because of it, provide some encouragement to someone else facing a similar circumstance.

The long and short of the matter is that God put us here for a reason. We don't exist in a vacuum. Every aspect of our lives should be a potential gift to the Lord and a blessing to His people. It's a waste of time and resources if we don't look for ways to make a difference for the Lord in this world. That is the heart of the message in this passage. Notice the Master looks to His servants to serve others. He expects kindness, love, compassion, and caring to abound from those who have received His promise. He is also not afraid to admonish and punish those of His servants who become neglectful and abusive.

Here are some important questions to consider. Have you been given much? Do you live comfortably? Have you achieved a position of status and authority? Have you been given talents that can make a difference in your life and the lives of others?

If you answered yes to any of these questions, you have a responsibility to fulfill for the Lord. Remember, however, you need to respond with humility and meekness. Some of the most successful people I know are also the kindest and most generous.

We serve a Lord who gave us all we have. We need to serve His people and share what we possess.

GOD HAS A VISION FOR YOU; HOW ABOUT YOU?

PROVERBS 4

P lan to live a hundred more years and live every day as if it were your last. It's wise advice I received once, and it still applies. It's very easy to get caught up in our daily routine. Unfortunately, when we do, we overlook opportunities and miss blessings the Lord has for us. We must monitor the normal routine of our lives, but we can't afford to get caught up to the extent we bypass new chances to serve the Lord and further His kingdom.

I am very goal-oriented person. I am not happy just thinking about today, for tomorrow holds such promise and opportunity. Looking forward to what could be enhances my motivation to be passionate about today. In Revelation, God complains to the church in Ephesus that they had lost their first love. It wasn't that they stopped believing; rather they lost their passion and vision. They were doing the right kinds of things, but they were unenthusiastic about them.

These combined passages give some insight into the heart of God. He is more than just passively interested in us and our future; He is overwhelmed with enthusiasm. God created us to enjoy life with Him. He is excited and passionate about us and the rest of His creation. Additionally I believe it is fair to say that He wants us to share His level of emotion. We were not created to be passive. We were created to be involved and dynamic additions to paradise. Adam and Eve were designed to take part in God's creation by enjoying its beauty and enhancing its intended purpose. Much as a master painter will put a fresh canvas and paint in the hands of his student, so God put the Garden of Eden in the hands of Adam and Eve.

You are a student under the direction of the Master. You have an opportunity to create a beautiful picture on the canvas of your life. The question is: do you see the work of art that could be? Have you taken a step back to consider the masterpiece hidden within, or are you caught up with what to do with the supplies you've been provided? Yours is an opportunity to take the life you've been given and turn it into something beautiful to behold. Yours is the chance of a lifetime to discover your potential and move relentlessly toward it.

We marvel at times about the achievements of others and wonder how they attained such success. For most, it was not an accident or the result of being lucky. Rather most were successful because they took the tools God gave them and became masters in their own right. Instead of waiting for opportunity to fall in their lap, they pursued it with passion and tenacity.

You are a work of art, the product of the master artist Himself. There are elements you need to contribute to the project: your heart, your passion, your ingenuity, and your love. You are not yet what you could be in Christ, but the masterpiece is there. It's your responsibility to see it and begin to paint it. Only when you act will the beauty of the picture unfold and begin to become what the Master intended.

BE CAREFUL OF THE SPIRITUAL ADVICE YOU GIVE; GOD IS LISTENING TOO

JOB 42:7–9

People love to give advice. They love to influence the actions of others based on their own personal experience and knowledge. Christians are no exception. God commanded us to love one another and to actively involve ourselves in each other's lives. The involvement is usually sourced from a caring heart and a genuine desire to do good things and make a positive difference. Quite frankly, our interaction with others adds a fulfilling measure to our daily existence, not to mention the potential benefit to the recipient of the information.

I have observed and find it troubling, however, that some Christians give advice from other than an experienced perspective. Indeed, sometimes their underlying motives are biased toward personal gain or ambitions rather than altruistic concerns for the person in need. Too often the advice given is couched in some spiritual sounding rhetoric, complete with a scripture verse that may or may not be in context. I've known some to even go so far as to begin their counsel with the phrase, "God told me …"

I know I am now stepping on some toes, but I'm concerned about the approach we take to assist one another when there is a possibility that we may not be acting from the direction of the Holy Spirit. It's very easy in this life to give advice or direction more from our human perspective or personal zeal, or at worst, a deception instigated by the enemy than from a completely unbiased point of view. It is easy to interject some of our personal desires about another's life into a situation where our ideas may actually be harmful to them.

I'm not saying we should not give advice. Knowledge and wisdom come most often from the perspective of someone who has been down the path already. What I am suggesting is we take the time to prayerfully consider the advice and direction we give to others to add assurance we are completely acting in their best interest.

Consider the story of Job. Job was a believer who was subjected to a significant test of his faith. The test was focused on proving the depth and veracity of Job's love for God. It was an overwhelmingly difficult test. During the test, perhaps as part of the test, Job's friends came to give him advice. Not only did they miss the point of what was actually happening, but they also began to accuse him of sins and other shortcomings they assumed (wrongly) to be at the core of Job's problems. It is troubling to recognize that the basis of Job's friends' criticisms was a shortsighted misunderstanding of God's Word and a completely false assumption regarding Job's faithfulness. Not only did Job's friends give him poor advice, but they became arrogant and indignant when Job wouldn't capitulate to their presumptuous observations.

At the end of the book, God scolds Job's friends and instructs them to look to Job to help them offer a sacrifice for their sins. Interestingly, God was only interested in hearing Job's prayer because He was angry at the presumptuous folly of their positions.

At the end of the day, we need to measure our words when we give them on God's behalf. We must remember He is listening and He doesn't appreciate when His children are misled because human pride and presumption get in the way of His love and compassion.

VISION AND PURPOSE ARE COMPANIONS OF PASSION AND JOY

PROVERBS 29:18

It is interesting how sometimes you have to lose something before you understand its importance. At times in my life, I feel like I've completely lost track of where I am and where I'm going. It's not that I'm not active or engaged; rather it's that I'm too busy or too spread out. I know I have purpose in my life, but I tend to lose focus because of distractions and concerns.

Most of us lead busy lives. We're stretched thin and pulled in multiple directions simultaneously. When this occurs, we begin to find ourselves increasingly frustrated and upset. Instead of each day bringing new opportunities to find joy, they offer only endless activity and demands on our time.

I've had seasons in my life when things seemed pretty pointless and discouraging. I wasn't moving measurably toward my goals, and my hopes and dreams seemed empty and distant. At times I never seemed to progress toward anything worthwhile. Instead life was overcome with cares and concerns pulling my heart toward discouragement and away from the Lord.

I'm not sure why such times come about or what to do about them. They seem to be a natural part of our existence here on this small planet. It just bothers me that I don't consistently live every day focused and motivated to move in the direction God has ordained for my life.

The Bible teaches that people without direction and purpose perish. Life becomes meaningless when we have no reason for being. When we find ourselves tied to endless activity, we begin to become discouraged and empty. Our days provide no satisfaction and joy. We lose hope. We lose desire. We lose peace.

So what do we do? How do we change directions? The answer is simpler than we may wish to admit. We simply have to decide to change. Just as we turn the corner in our car, we take hold of the wheel and change direction. It's our choice. We don't rely on others to do it for us, although some may want to help. We just decide to take a new tack and change our heading.

Even at that, we still have to do one other thing. We have to decide where we are going. Purpose and vision require something to focus upon. Changing directions for change's sake will still leave us distressed and down. Moving in a direction toward a specific goal or objective will fill us with passion and joy.

We were not designed to be aimless creatures wandering the world endlessly, living pointlessly activity-filled days. We were designed for a reason with purpose and direction impacting everything we do. Find purpose. Find joy. Gain vision. Realize passion. Do everything to the glory of God so your life increases in value and peace.

YOUR HAPPINESS WILL NOT BE IMPACTED BY YOUR CIRCUMSTANCES IF YOU'RE A MACHINE!

PSALM 71

Perhaps you've heard Christians should always be joyful, celebrating life at every turn regardless of their circumstances. Maybe you've gone to church and seen all of the smiling faces of the people who always seem to be living well-ordered, prosperous lives. I've read books and listened to sermons reminding me to be joyful in the face of trials and tests. Time and time again, I have endured difficulties and problems beyond my ability to control or change. I have to confess. I didn't feel too happy at those times. Indeed, I felt downright lousy.

I've known the Lord for the better part of my life. Over the years, I've learned that He is absolutely faithful. He has always been there for me and seen me through all of the problems that came my way. Interestingly, in the heat of the battle, He didn't leave me, but I didn't always feel like He was at my side either. It's an unusual feeling. On the one hand, I feel lost and forgotten. On the other hand, I have an uncanny certainty that in the end all will be well and I will see His hand at work. It's my experience with Him over the years that gives me more confidence when each new trial comes. I'm not necessarily happy when the problems show up, but I can approach them with a greater degree of confidence that He will be faithful. This faithfulness is a source of joy for me.

What about the rest of how I feel? The rest of how I feel is real. It's honest. It's heartfelt, and it's not always happy. Moreover, I am less concerned about expressing the negative side of my emotions directly to the Lord. I've spent more time over the last few years reading the Psalms. If you really look at them closely, you will find they contain a wide cross-section of human emotions. They express everything from joy and exuberance to anger and complete despair. Additionally there are no apologies for the honest emotions they contain. The psalmists simply poured their hearts out to the Lord. They told Him how they felt point-blank, with no candy coating or soft stepping. They were not even afraid to express anger or question the Lord's apparent lack of involvement.

How many times have I felt like that? I've found myself feeling neglected and alone, but I was afraid to express it to my Father who loves me. I always feared I was being irreverent if I expressed any disappointing thought to God, particularly when I felt He was the source of the disappointment. No longer! Studying the Psalms and reading books about them has helped me understand the depth of God's concern for my predicament. God is not afraid of how I feel. He is not put off by the fact I get angry or distressed. Indeed God wants to know how I feel. He wants to know the true condition of my heart. Why? Simple! That's where He meets me. That's the place where I finally drop my guard and show Him my true colors. Also, that is the place I learn to trust Him the most. A true friend is someone who loves you regardless of your circumstances—happy, sad, glad, and indifferent. Ultimately, I can be who I truly am with the Lord with no airs and no pretenses. The joy I have in the Lord doesn't require me to be continuously happy. In fact, the joy is substantiated the most when I am sad; for you see, that's when God holds me the closest.

GOD'S MERCY IS MEASURELESS; ABOUT LIKE MY NEED FOR IT

PSALM 30

There are days, and there are days. Have you ever had days when you feel like you are in the doldrums? You know, days that seem to be filled with listlessness, not bad but not necessarily great either. I hate when days like that come up. I tend to be unproductive and off my game. Instead of being passionate about the possibilities the day holds, I would just as soon let time pass me by without accomplishing much of anything. I feel out of sorts and neglectful.

I was having one of those days today. There was a variety of things happening around me, but none of them touched my heart, at least until a few moments ago. I think God knew I needed a wake-up call because He sent me one. I received an email unexpectedly with a beautiful Christian message that just went straight to my heart. It was amazing and surprising all at the same time.

I imagine this seems like such a little thing, but it made a big difference to me. I serve a God who is concerned about my well-being, whether I'm on the mountaintop, in the valley, or wandering around somewhere in between. The funny thing is I spend most of my life in between, so knowing He's there at those times gives me more confidence about the other times. The lesson for me is simple: God cares. Big issue or small issue, it doesn't matter. God cares. I tend to wonder sometimes if I really do matter to the Lord, and an experience like this convinces me of His passionate love.

Every day, we all need the Lord. Now we may find it easy to overlook that fact, but it is one of the most important things we need to know. Our need for Him transcends everything else in life. Regardless of whether we have been seeking a closer walk with Him or not, He is there. He waits for us, walks with us, leads us, and even comes and gets us when we lose our way. He's never afraid to love me, correct me, encourage me, or even shake me from time to time. I wonder if He's there only to find He's been with me the whole time.

What is most amazing is His willingness to forgive and love me when I do things that disappoint Him. None of us is perfect, and I am a prime example of that fact. I hate to fail Him, but at times it feels like that's my primary profession. I hate it, but it's the way things are. Yet through it all, God demonstrates His mercy to me and helps me to move toward fulfilling His plan for my life.

Mercy is a simple and a life-changing word. It tells us there is hope when we feel there is none. With God, the mercy flows freely to those who love Him. I do love Him, but I will never deserve Him. I guess that's why it's called mercy in the first place. It's an undeserved gift given to the needy and the lost; you know, people just like you and me. I need God's mercy, and He gives it in overflowing portions, not just to me, but to anyone who asks.

WHEN IT SEEMS GOD DIDN'T ANSWER YOUR PRAYER, DID YOU CONSIDER HE MAY JUST HAVE SAID NO?

PSALM 4

Where are you, Lord? I pray, and sometimes it seems like the Lord is taking the day off. I don't know if you've ever experienced that, but most of my friends have, and I certainly have. I wonder sometimes if God is truly listening and really cares about me. I bring Him my cares and concerns with the hope He will help me solve them. Unfortunately, I often feel I'm not getting through. It's hard to understand. God has promised to answer my prayers, and I know His Word is true, so what's going on?

I have wrestled with this issue numerous times in my life. I expect I will wrestle with it again. Through it all, I have learned some things that only a long-term relationship can reveal. First and foremost, God has proved His faithfulness. I know this may seem incongruous based on my earlier statements, but it's true. Simply put, God's timing usually does not match my own, but it is always complementary to my needs. Looking back on my life, I can see how He has responded to my pleas, often in ways I would never have expected or hoped. You see, God is responding to your prayers even now, but he may be doing it at a pace or in a way you cannot discern. The twists and turns of my life illustrate God's involvement at every moment. He has taken me places I never anticipated going. He has also given me experiences I never would have considered or contemplated.

Knowing God is faithful helps me to understand another aspect of my prayer life. It is an element that is sometimes frustrating and often difficult to understand. Simply put, sometimes God says no. Hard to believe? I've often thought so, but it's true just the same. I've read books and listened to sermons about prayer that tend to suggest God is a great big sugar daddy, just waiting to fulfill our every wish and whim. It doesn't work that way. God has a plan for my life and a plan for this world. He is executing that plan according to His sovereign will and purpose for His creation. I am merely a small component in that overall design, so my life and desires need to fit into that program.

So where does that leave us when it comes to our prayer life and God's impact on our lives? First and foremost, we need to remember God loves us personally and intimately. When we bring our needs and desires to Him, He listens and lovingly responds. Second, we need to remember God understands the entirety of our life and His plan for us. Consequently He is going to respond from that context. We can know He is going to lovingly move us in a direction that is in our best interest and conforms to His universal plan for the world. Finally, we need to understand God reserves the right to say no. If you are a parent, you will understand this pretty readily. Sometimes we just tend to ask for things that are outside of God's plan; other times we ask for things that might be good, but for which we are not ready. Any way you cut it, God remains sovereign. He is ruler over all!

Look to the Lord for all of the needs of your life. Bring every concern and hope in your heart to our Father who loves you. Pray to develop your relationship with Him, and through it all, seek a life more devoted to His service. Above all, remember God is faithful, and His mercy endures forever.

TRIALS TEST YOUR CONVICTIONS

JAMES 1:1–18

I don't like trials and tests. Oh, I know that trials are a necessary part of life. It's just that they can be so unsettling and disturbing. Let's face it. Very few of us look forward to our next trial. In fact, if we didn't have to face another trial, that would be just fine. Well, the best response I can give to that feeling is to forget about it. Trials are coming your way. It's just a question of where and when, not if.

What does that mean to us? How are we supposed to respond to tests and trials when they come? Believe it or not, it's not just a grin-and-bear-it situation. We don't need to sit around waiting for the other shoe to fall on another problem. Certainly problems come, but through it all, we need to realize something, that God loves us.

Adversity and frustrations, while difficult to cope with, bring with them the opportunity to learn something new and to grow. Much of life is a series of tests designed to help us to develop into the person God designed us to be. To move toward the mark God has set for us, we need to progress past where we are to a place we may never have gone. Many people have gone on to achieve great things in their lives only after they faced a great or potentially overwhelming trial. Nevertheless, it's hard to persevere. Perhaps that's one of the things God intends to teach us.

Perseverance is one of the more difficult things you will attempt to do in your life. It requires commitment, patience, love, passion, courage, tenacity, and energy. When it is put to the test, you will be tempted to give up, throw up your hands, and walk away. That's exactly what the Lord does not want you to do. Instead He wants you to rise to the challenge, trust in Him, and press on.

None of these actions are easy to take, and all of them will go directly to the very nature of who you are as a person. You need to consider that the Lord is preparing you to be everything you were designed to be. You can't become the best you without addressing the issues God brings across your path.

Finally, there is one more important element you must be wary of if you're to succeed. Do not allow yourself to become discouraged. Now, I know that is easier said than done, but it is a significant element of your success. Overcoming discouragement is your ticket to contentment and achievement. Obviously there are no guarantees in life. Even if you work hard, you may not overcome, but overcome you must.

Loving the Lord is ultimately a question of remaining committed to your faith even when the chips are down. When it seems nothing could possibly go your way, God will provide a way to carry on. He may not remove your burden, but He will share it. In a nutshell, that is exactly what the Lord wants. He wants you to look for Him in every situation you face and allow Him to help you through. That is the way of faith, and that is your source of faith in a trial.

SO WHAT'S THE ADVANTAGE TO NOT KNOWING CHRIST?

HEBREWS 3

You will have to explain this one to me because, to be honest, I've never understood it. Why do people perceive there is an advantage to not believing in Christ? Why do they rail against the notion that God exists and that He created the universe? What's wrong with the idea God loves us and sent His Son to die on a cross for us? Is there a disadvantage to eternal life?

I've listened to people in the media, the scientific community, academia, and other backgrounds argue long and loud about their disbelief in God. They cite numerous reasons based upon their interpretation of the facts they see in life as to why they shouldn't believe. Interestingly, when subjected to closer scrutiny, their facts are flawed or their bent on them is simply biased toward an underlying desire not to believe in the first place.

I could write entire books on the numerous points of disagreement between evangelical believers and those who choose to disregard God. Certainly, store shelves are filled with texts on numerous topics either supporting or refusing faith in God. Obviously I would be on the side of those who believe, but I have one significant question for those who argue so passionately against the faith. What's the advantage of a nonbelieving position? What possible benefit exists that could matter one million years from today to not believing? Quite frankly, I don't believe one exists!

Think about it. If you throw out the Bible, you throw out the Ten Commandments and the rule of law. Actually it's worse. You throw out any basis for moral values of any kind. No longer are there underlying reasons for love, hope, peace, joy, or mercy. No longer does it matter whether we gain knowledge or survive the day. Instead of working to improve our lives and the lives of those around us, there becomes no basis for learning, development, or wisdom. Nothing matters because, in the final analysis, nothing lasts.

Absent belief in God, there is no reason to succeed or fail; no reason to do anything. While instinctive behaviors may suggest otherwise, there is no rational reason for an ordered society if there is no underlying reason for order in the first place. Any position on any issue is fully defensible absent Christ. Since there would be no direct moral compass for any action, any action or inaction would suffice. What's worse, life would ultimately be meaningless, providing no hope for the future and no valid rewards for positive behavior. Simply put, positive behavior could not happen because there would be no rational definition of either positive or negative.

The end result of disbelief is emptiness. Life, if you could call it that, would simply degenerate into a mindless series of events having neither purpose nor direction. There would be no hope because hope comes from faith. There would be no joy, no peace, and no good. Life would be a stream of meaningless events, nothing to look forward to, nothing that matters.

So really, what's the advantage to not knowing Christ?

IT'S HARD TO GET ENERGIZED IF YOU'RE NOT PLUGGED IN!

HEBREWS 10:15–25

There is safety in numbers, not to mention enthusiasm, energy, encouragement, and strength; all positive attributes we can each find helpful as we make our way in this world. Moving successfully through life in any respect is, by necessity, a group effort. While you may be excellent at a particular discipline or skill, input and assistance from others usually enhances your results and helps you maintain your edge.

It's a funny thing about church. Most Christians will agree it is a positive thing, but most will also look for reasons not to attend or become involved. Many of us will claim to have the desire to improve as individuals, but we will stop short of becoming actively involved in church. It's easy to become complacent about our faith, particularly as it relates to getting together with other Christians. When Sunday rolls around, we are ready for some rest, so getting up early to get together with other members of the body may not be as appealing as rolling over and switching off the alarm. Nevertheless, it's an essential part of moving forward with your faith while mitigating some of the risks of living in this world.

Life is full of detours, holdups, wrong turns, and switchbacks. We will often find ourselves moving along at what we consider a reasonable pace, only to come upon a problem that returns us to square one. In the twinkling of an eye, our whole world can be turned upside down, leaving us exasperated and alone. God did not intend for us to go it alone, however. He knew we would face trials and difficulties, causing us to question the purpose of our life and our ability to go on.

Church is focused on encouraging one another every bit as much as it relates to teaching us about the Savior we love. Contained in the second great commandment enumerated by Christ is the notion that we should support and encourage one another. Even going back to Adam and Eve at the beginning of Genesis reveals a human need for companionship and love.

At the end of the day, church is not about what you wear or where you sit. It's about worshipping and glorifying God and loving and supporting each other.

God's name must be exalted among us, but we can't effectively achieve that if we fail to assemble for this purpose. Being a hermit only makes you alone, but it doesn't make you a better Christian. You may be very strong in your faith and feel you can make it on your own, but consider for a moment that Christ was the strongest of us all, and He consistently met with other believers to teach and encourage them. Additionally Christ sought out other believers for support when He faced the darkest moments of His life.

Keep the faith by staying involved. Don't give up on your fellow Christians because you need each other. Even if you are singularly strong in your faith, there may be others who need some encouragement from you. Besides, the day may come when you're the one who needs the help, and if you're already plugged in, you won't be too far away from the help you need.

READ THE WORD IN CONTEXT; TEACH THE WORD IN LOVE

2 CORINTHIANS 4

I like to use longer scripture passages to support my lessons and devotionals. I use the expanded text to better explain the intent of the key passage relative to the issue being examined. It has long been a concern of mine that many people try to manipulate the Scriptures, taking them out of context in order to support an idea that might not otherwise fit with the Word. Christ tells us in Matthew to watch out for those who would attempt to deceive us before His return. His prophetic message is proving out in our world today.

I don't have the experience of having lived in other eras. Accordingly I can't honestly say that this age is any better or worse when it comes to how the gospel is presented. We know for a fact there have been faithful Christ-loving people around ever since Christ's ascension. We also know the enemy has been actively opposing the spread of the gospel during this same period. Good faces off against evil still today, and the fight is ours to pursue.

I am writing this to encourage you to take time to learn the Word of God and gain an appropriate understanding of the Lord's message to us. I have been a student of the Bible since I was in my teens, but I have to confess there have been seasons of my life when I did not pay as much attention to the Word as I should. Today I am more consistently reading and studying when and where I can, which brings me back to the subject at hand.

You can't know what the Bible really says unless you read it for yourself. When you do, you will find some wonderful things. You may also come across some surprises and some questions. All of these are good and profitable for your relationship with Christ. Moreover, you will have direct knowledge of the truth and will be less likely to be deceived. Finally, seeking resolution to the new questions you have should prompt further study and examination of the facts, which will lead to a closer walk with the Lord.

In my experience, I have come across people who have told me God specifically told them something, only later to find out it was more their personal zeal speaking rather than the Lord. I've also heard preachers claim to have a special revelation from God, yet the message didn't tie in with scripture, even when they quoted several diverse verses to support their ideas.

I'm not telling you that God doesn't or can't speak to people. He's God. He can do whatever He wants. What I am telling you to do is to use the same tests the apostles said to use. Test the message against the Word of God; pray and patiently wait upon the Lord. If the message is true, it will line up with Scripture and be confirmed by prayer and the test of time. Finally, the benefit of the message will ultimately glorify God in all respects.

God is not afraid of us asking questions in an honest attempt to follow His will. In fact, I would suggest to you that He encourages us to do so. But He also desires for us to use the brain He gave us to rightly divide the truth so we will not be misled; nor will we tend to mislead others.

JOB DIDN'T LOSE HIS FAITH; HE PROVED IT

JOB 42

Sometimes I think I have it so tough. I gripe and complain and find all kinds of reasons why life should be better. While I've never gotten to the point of being so angry with God that I was shaking my fist at Him, I do have to admit to being very disappointed with His handling of things. I question God regularly because I don't understand why circumstances impact me and my plans so negatively. Furthermore, my troubles seem to be amplified by the positive events that seem to more frequently visit other people. But is it really that way?

Throughout my life, I've encountered difficulties and setbacks that at the time seemed overwhelming and exasperating. I was never quite prepared for them, and I was frustrated and annoyed. I seem to suffer from the "this shouldn't be happening to me" syndrome. I presume you may have encountered this malady over the years as well. If so, you probably understand the associated emotions. I wish there were a cure for it, but it seems to recur without warning. I hate it, or maybe it's just the events that lead to an outbreak that I don't like.

Thank heaven for Job! I wish I could have met him. The poor guy was minding his own business when everything in his life began to fall apart. It wasn't just a few mild setbacks either. He lost his kids, possessions, health, and even the support of his friends. His wife even got to the point that she told him to "curse God and die!" (Job 2:9); not exactly the level of loving support one might desire when the whole world is falling down around one's ears.

The worst part was Job's friends. They provided a circle of support much akin to a noose. With all of the compassion of a mudslide, they moved from being supportive counselors to prosecutors, judges, and juries. Oh, they meant well, at least at first, but later they took it upon themselves to take God's place as pillars of the faith determined to bring the rogue believer back into the fold. Instead of support, they brought Job condemnation. Instead of blessing, they offered a curse. Instead of love, they brought disdain.

Job suffered it all, but there was one thing his supporters didn't consider. Circumstances do not dictate the condition of one's heart. Job did not sin and bring calamity upon himself; the calamity came from an outside source. Additionally, while Job suffered immeasurably, the suffering was not a sign of faithlessness. Job suffered because he was attacked. Job overcame the attack because his faith never wavered. God blessed Job because Job's faithfulness was an example to us all.

Job's faith was initially strong and finally immovable. He overcame adversity and taught us all how to stand. In the end, he was commended by God and blessed beyond anything he previously knew. As for his friends, their prideful self-righteous speeches proved to be their undoing. The lessons for us? Be faithful to God, for He is always faithful to you. Cling to God's love because it transcends our understanding. Don't presume to know the mind of God when all you can see are circumstances beyond your control.

PRIDE COMES BEFORE THE FALL; IT'S THE THING MOST PEOPLE TRIP OVER FIRST!

PROVERBS 11:1–10

I can't tell you how many times I've seen it happen, a prideful person falling into one of the enemy's traps and being utterly destroyed. The failures cross all boundaries in both the secular and Christian world. The trap of pride can impact something as simple as a ballgame or as complicated as the destiny of human life. Pride often occurs after spectacular successes but can also crop up with those who fail. Pride points to the self and says, "I'm better; I can overcome anyone; I always come out on top." Pride is myopic because the focus is always internal. It ignores the needs of others and is the root cause of offenses.

Interestingly, God is particularly offended by pride. Indeed the Bible tells us that God hates pride. Moreover, time and again the Bible tells how God is going to destroy the proud people and bring them to humility. Understanding God's greatness and absolute power, it's easy to see why He would be offended by people who are full of themselves. This brings me to an important question: If God hates pride and admonishes us against it, why do we so often find it in the church?

It's distressing to know how negatively pride impacts our faith and ability to minister to others. Pride keeps us from admitting our faults, and it inhibits our willingness to answer God's promptings. Pride makes us feel holier than thou and prevents us from accepting those we perceive as less spiritual than ourselves. Pride is active in our churches primarily because we fail to give it much attention. We accept people at face value rather than note that none of us come to the Lord deserving His favor.

Most of us recognize the pride statements in church but fail to see them for what they are; sin. Most of the "I" statements you hear have a great risk of being prideful, particularly the ones followed by the phrase "don't like." Much worse, however, are the attitudes that quickly condemn people who have become involved in publicly known sins. Visible sin is easily judged, and those caught up in it often become victims twice, first with the sin and second at the hands of those who would condemn them for it.

Churches are not perfect places, and they are all attended by people who themselves are not perfect. The risk is that some of those attending see themselves through prideful clouds of delusion, thus opening themselves up to a fall and potentially harming the faith of others. Numerous times through the years I've heard stories about important Christian leaders being caught up in sexual sin. There are embarrassing headlines followed by shattered churches and individual lives. While the excuses are many, ultimately pride enters the equation. It may be a root cause of the sin of the fallen person or may come in the judgmental response of the rest of the church itself.

Any way you cut it, pride destroys. It eats its victims for lunch and often consumes numerous innocent bystanders for dessert. Pride is a devious enemy, and we need to be wary of its devices, particularly when in comparison to Christ, we have very little to be prideful about.

DON'T BE SO BUSY BEING OFFENDED WHEN THERE'S A RELATIONSHIP TO BE MENDED

GENESIS 27, GENESIS 32, AND GENESIS 33:1–11

"I'm sorry," a simple phrase really, a small collection of words, is just a few syllables in length. It's surprising just how difficult it is to say these words, particularly if we have to mean them. The message is easy enough to understand and not complicated to communicate, yet it can be impossible to utter even for the most courageous among us.

Along with "I love you," these words have the potential to change the course of relationships, opening up new vistas of grandeur and beauty previously thought impossible. But if we never take that path we can never know the beauty that awaits us.

There is a disturbing tendency in our society today that is the antithesis of a spirit of forgiveness and reconciliation. It is the desire to seek retribution for wrongs incurred. We have developed the notion that for every wrong we suffer, there must be just compensation. Every loss sustained, regardless of its source, must be recovered along with additional punishing compensation designed to exact the maximum amount of pain upon the party behind the offense.

Gone are the days of forgiveness and love. Today we look for a lawyer to solve our differences rather than working them out between ourselves. Instead of seeking reconciliation through a discussion with our neighbor, we seek compensation by raiding his pocketbook. Instead of rekindling a lifelong friendship, we create an enemy with whom we may never speak again. The sad part is that this approach slowly undermines our lives, making us increasingly bitter and hateful instead of loving and joyful.

Saying "I'm sorry" is becoming a lost art, and as it fades it takes peace and harmony with it. Now don't get me wrong. When somebody does something wrong, I believe they should do everything in their power to make things right. Indeed the Bible teaches we should compensate people several times over for the losses they sustain at our hands. The important thing is we need to recognize and accept this responsibility when it is ours. Likewise, we need to accept apologies when sincerely offered and look for ways to encourage reconciliation with others when the opportunity arises.

We don't live in a perfect world, and none of us are perfect people. All of us find ways to hurt others and fall well short of being perfect people. Recognizing this situation and accepting the truth of it puts us in a better frame of mind to come up with positive responses when things go awry.

Loving others and forgiving them for their failings requires more effort and energy than the alternative. It is not effort and energy expended with no potential benefits. Investing yourself in the lives of others will bring you fulfillment and joy. Learning to reconcile differences and reestablish relationships is a key component of peace and contentment vital to a complete life in Christ.

DO MORE THAN GET YOUR FEET WET; ASK THE DEEP QUESTIONS

PROVERBS 2

Our family went to the beach a short time ago. It was just a quick stop while we were vacationing in Washington state. It was a cool day, so none of us were motivated to jump into the water. There was just enough time to take our shoes off so we could walk along and get our feet wet as the waves rolled in. It was a wonderful day. The scenery was breathtaking. We were together as a family and had not a care in the world. It was the break we all needed.

I love vacation days where my biggest worry is how late I can sleep and what I am going to eat next. Days like that are a respite from the rest of life that brings pressures and schedules, constant attention to detail, and responsibility for who knows what. The reality is that most of my life is about achieving goals, raising my kids, and planning for the future. It keeps me busy. At times it's stressful, and I like it. It makes me dig deep to try to achieve all I can while still keeping everything in balance.

Balance, that's the key. In this life, in our world, it's easy to let things get out of balance. We tend to focus on quick and easy solutions rather than approaching tough problems head-on. We tend to go on vacation permanently because doing so allows us to ignore the tough questions life throws our way. Unfortunately this approach sells us short and leaves us with few options when things go against us. Not only is this true in our day-to-day lives, it's true in our spiritual lives as well. Too often we back away from the tough questions of our faith, ending up with a minimal understanding of some very important concepts.

We have been placed in this world by God to love Him, love others, and spread the gospel message. We can't spread the message very effectively if we don't fully understand it ourselves. Moreover, it's easier to be misled when someone twists Scripture to suit their personal agenda if we don't have the background necessary to ferret out the truth. I'm not saying we all need to be biblical scholars, although that would be nice. I'm saying we need to be attentive to the important issues of our faith so we can base our lives on a reliable understanding of God's Word.

The key is that we should always be seeking to learn. We should ask the questions we can't sort out on our own, and we should not be afraid to put someone on the spot. Christ was never afraid to confront any question put to Him. He not only demonstrated His understanding of Scripture, but He also answered within the context of the attitude and agenda of the person asking. We need to be prepared as well. We cannot be satisfied with candy-coated, one-size-fits-all answers to people's questions.

In the end, we need to approach our faith with the same level of intensity we would give to our important daily decisions and activities. We can't take the walk-along-the-beach approach to the important questions of our faith. We must do more than just get our feet wet. We need to jump in and immerse ourselves in our faith, for when we do, we will add strength and consistency to our walk. Not to mention, we will be better equipped to approach others with the love of our Savior Jesus Christ.

MARK WILKEN

WHILE WE KNOW THEY MADE IT ON THE ARK, MOOSE ARE NEVER MENTIONED IN THE BIBLE

2 TIMOTHY 3

Moose are neat animals. Thinking of them conjures up images of pristine mountain scenes in faraway places, unless, of course, you live near the moose. They're big animals and somewhat funny looking. I've never met one personally, but I've been told they can be pretty aggressive. I know you will find this fascinating, but a word search for any references related to moose in the entire text of the Bible will not yield one word about them.

So what conclusions can we draw from this apparent scriptural oversight? The answer, although somewhat startling at first, is simple; None! As far as I can determine, there is no relevant conclusion we can draw about the absence of moose in scripture. Some people, I'm afraid, may conclude something different with potentially disturbing implications. For example, some may conclude that moose are not a relevant part of God's creation since they are not mentioned, even though God did take the time to create them. Others might conclude there is something sinister about moose resulting in their omission from the scriptural text. Finally, some may postulate that moose don't really exist because they are not a component of the scriptural record. Certainly the mention of moose was not an oversight, or was it?

Before you decide I've completely lost my marbles, there is something I would like you to consider. The Bible was never intended to be a complete unabridged encyclopedia of every life experience, every biological, scientific, or mathematical fact people can possibly conceive. It is not intended to answer every theoretical concept we can devise; nor is it an exhaustive treatise regarding geopolitical relations. Funny, but a lot of people treat it that way.

For some in the church, the Bible serves as a benchmark for life that removes all thought (and therefore, responsibility) from daily life. If the Bible addresses an issue, they will address the issue. If the Bible is silent about an issue, they will attempt to ignore or avoid it. They seem to want to live on a spiritual island instead of confronting real-life issues head-on.

In the world, the problem is different. Critics of the Bible, particularly those who haven't read it, contend its silence on issues renders it useless and unreliable. According to some of them, the fact that the Bible doesn't exhaustively discuss scientific issues reveals that it is fatally flawed. The omission, for example, of discussions about climate change proves that Christians are out of touch with the concerns of our natural environment.

The imbalance of both of the above-described problems should be obvious. The Bible has to be studied from the context of what it was intended to be. The Bible is not an exhaustive research volume for scientific reference purposes; rather it's a love letter from God the Father to us. While it does contain some scientific, geopolitical, and mathematical facts, it was designed more for us to use as a guide for how to find Christ and what to do with our lives. The Bible is our guide for life, and we should use it as such. It is not, however, the sum total of all of God's thoughts; nor was it intended to be.

IF CHRISTIANITY BECOMES ILLEGAL, WILL YOU GET CONVICTED?

MATTHEW 24:1–14

I don't know if you've noticed or not, but Christianity is no longer warmly received in this world. If you watch the news, popular TV programs, movies, or simply read the newspaper, you will find the Christian faith derided and maligned. Christian principles are mocked as being old-fashioned, backward, insensitive, obtuse, or simply ridiculous. Instead of seeing Christians as kind and loving, the world sees us as cold and indifferent. Moreover, we're considered out of touch with reality and just plain hypocritical. Not exactly the résumé most of us seek, is it?

There are times when I consider this problem, and it really begins to bother me. Honestly, I don't want people to think negatively of me or my faith. I want folks to understand the love of Christ and know the joy of having a personal relationship with a heavenly Father who loves them. It's sad. Not only do people avoid the Christian faith, they actively oppose it, even to the point of becoming violent. The world is increasingly openly hostile to Christ and His followers. It's a fact of our lives, and we need to be ready.

I'm not writing this to discourage or dishearten someone. I'm writing it to encourage and prepare. Christ taught His followers about the end times. When He did, He was candid and straightforward. He didn't beat around the bush, and He didn't pull any punches. His disciples knew they faced a hostile world and an enemy out to thwart their efforts. Christ's message was meant to prepare the disciples for the difficulties that would lie ahead.

The question for us is: when our turn comes and adversity and hostility call, will we stand firm or run out the back door? I've often wondered, if armed troops showed up at our churches some Sunday in order to prevent the worship services from happening, would we fall away or worship anyway? It's an important question and one every Christian needs to be prepared to answer. Christ warned us that standing up for the faith would become increasingly difficult as the end times approached. We must heed that warning and steel our hearts for what could be coming soon to a church near you.

Now I don't claim to have any special insight into the timing of the end times. Christ Himself didn't know when the day of the Lord would be. There is really only one certainty about it. It will happen at a moment of God's choosing. The key for us as Christians is to be prepared and also to be proactive. We know about the end times so we can know we have hope. We know about the end times so we can be prepared. We know about the end times so we will not be casual about spreading the Word about our faith, even at the cost of our earthly lives. The disciples stood even in the face of death. Christ stood even in the face of death. What about us?

IT'S NOT NECESSARILY ABOUT BLACK AND WHITE AS MUCH AS IT'S ABOUT BALANCE

1 CORINTHIANS 10:23–33

Rules. Christians love rules. We have written and unwritten rules. We have acceptable and unacceptable practices. I think we even have laws and rumors of laws. Then come the grey area issues. Most of these relate to activities and beliefs not specifically spelled out in the Bible but encountered in everyday life by most normal people. It seems most of the grey area issues fall on the side of don'ts: don't drink, don't smoke, don't wear jeans to church, don't interrupt the sermon with a question, and so on.

The list of do nots, should nots, and ought nots would fill several volumes if accumulated from churches around America. Indeed, I believe they would rival the Internal Revenue Code for complexity and rigidity. Moreover, this set of rules is irrevocable and unchangeable, except and unless someone would like to add to the list, thereby improving it.

You may think that I am overstating the case just a bit, but too often it feels like the rules of Christendom far outweigh the opportunities. Essentially, God designed us to be much, much more than rule followers and teetotalers. In fact, when you focus on the teachings of Christ and the other biblical teachers, you find much more information about what we should be doing and what we should consider important. The guidance the Bible gives provides us the tools necessary to touch lives and change our world.

Now, it's obvious that we are a people called apart to do our Father's will. That is our job, but the job is founded in freedom not constrained by chains. We are certainly told what we should and should not do within the context of ministering and witnessing to others. Many of the things we should focus on are quite clear. It's what we do when we are operating in areas not specifically delineated in the Word that often cause consternation.

In my experience, I've learned to respond to others with love, compassion, and balance. Love and compassion are pretty obviously lined out for us in the Bible. It's the balance part that's more difficult to manage. All of us have a sense of right and wrong. This sense or conscience guides us regarding how we live and interact with others. The problem is that all of us have different sensibilities about what is acceptable versus what is not. When guidance exists in Scripture, most of us Christians line up pretty closely. The differences start with the issues not completely defined or which may vary when the related circumstances change. In these cases, Paul teaches us to develop a sense of balance. There may be good theological reasons for either doing or not doing something. The question is: does the action promote a holy and balanced life before the Lord? Additionally, does the issue enhance or degrade my relationship with Christ? The Bible doesn't say do not eat, but it does say not to be a glutton. What's the difference? Balance!

Simply put, things in our lives that pull us off balance expose us to the risk of falling into sin, even if we are off balance on the side of following the rules. Remember, the Pharisees were great at following and setting rules, but Christ noted on many occasions how far these men were from the Lord. In the end, Christ taught us to balance our lives on the Word of God working in our hearts to do the things we were called to do.

HANDS OFF DOESN'T WORK

PROVERBS 14:23

God's work has not been completed in this world. Indeed the needs are immeasurable and perpetual. Every day when you open the newspaper, there is a new story about the age-old problems of need, heartache, pain, and neglect. Few of the issues are new, but all of them are distressing. Some of the stories contain accounts of kindness where someone interjected themselves into the situation and made a difference. Sadly, however, these accounts are so few that we consider such individuals as heroes and we marvel at their daring actions.

My question is: where are we? More specifically, where is the church? While there is some church involvement in some of the situations, for the most part, we seem to be conspicuously absent. Now don't get me wrong. I'm probably the most conspicuously absent of all. That, however, is the problem. We in the church too easily take a holiday and forfeit opportunities to reach out to others. A sad result is that too few people now see the church as a place of comfort and assistance.

Throughout my life, it seems that the church has withdrawn from its former position as a community leader. It used to be common to hear of churches starting hospitals, opening shelters, reaching out to the homeless, and involving themselves in the problems of the community. When I was very young, it wasn't uncommon for Christians to be involved in public office, pursuing policies beneficial and loving to all.

To a certain degree, some of this still happens. However, it seems each year brings fewer instances of professing Christians assuming proactive roles in society. It's not that the church is totally absent; it's just not prevalent. For too long we have allowed others to assume the responsibility for confronting the woes of our communities and nation. We have moved our focus to the internal needs of the church and those who come through the doors but have increasingly withdrawn from the community at large.

There are many reasons for this situation to exist, some of them reasonable and others not. Certainly there has been increasing criticism of the church and faith in Christ. Today, true faith is increasingly shunned by the mainstream of society, not to mention being the brunt of jokes and derision in the entertainment community. Very few of the proactive programs the church pursues function without critics and skeptics.

Unfortunately, the church's response to such criticism has too often been to withdraw and focus within because being proactive in the community under the scrutiny of the media and other antagonists has become increasingly difficult. No longer can we just focus on trying to do the right thing, but we must do it with critics and scoffers deriding our efforts. The intense pressure for many years pushed us toward a hands-off response, but that can no longer be an acceptable approach. God brought us into this world to minister the truth, even when doing so is unpopular or openly ridiculed. We cannot be hands-off. We must have the courage to dig in and achieve for the Lord, going to the unpopular and uncomfortable places. When we do, we'll change lives and open more hearts to the truth of the gospel.

MARK WILKEN

I DON'T KNOW IF I COULD BE SO FORGIVING IF SOMEONE HUNG MY KID ON A CROSS

JOHN 19:1–37

The universe is a big place with lots of stars and planets and plenty of room to expand. Within that universe is a small planet known as Earth. It circles an ordinary star, and while it is quite attractive, it is not something God couldn't replicate should He be so disposed. On this planet reside many people groups placed here by a Creator who loves them. He breathed life into them, gave them all they needed to live, and allowed them to choose whether they would love Him back. It's an interesting arrangement if you think about it.

Over time, the people chose to do their own thing; in other words, they did the one thing the Creator asked them not to do, thereby rejecting His authority and love and their relationship. Funny thing is, while it was their right to do the wrong thing, the decision and result were both detrimental. To make matters worse, their descendants not only continued to choose to do the wrong thing, but they rejected the Creator outright. God was heartbroken by the loss of His relationship with His created people and set about to redeem them through an incredible sacrifice. He offered His Son to die for them.

Christ entered the world to bring salvation and redemption from the results of sin. His message is simple, easy to understand, and easy to accept. Christ's message was not just a collection of good words; rather it was a sacrifice that satisfied God's perfect law without compromising its foundations. Here's the extraordinary part. God let the very people He intended to save to kill the Redeemer, Jesus Christ. The plan of God required shed blood to satisfy perfection. Ironically, those who would shed Jesus' blood ultimately had the opportunity to be saved by it.

The people of this planet, the object of God's love, tortured and killed the Son. They hung Him on a cross with nails after practically beating Him to death first. From my perspective, it's strange, but God let them do it! He let them kill His kid. His love was so complete He was willing to make the ultimate sacrifice to reopen the door between Himself and us. Astounding!

I think sometimes what I would have done if someone treated my kid that way, if I had the power to intervene and stop the pain and suffering inflicted on my boy. Honestly, I think I would have rescued my son and zapped the planet into oblivion. I wouldn't have shown restraint, and I wouldn't have had any remorse. I would have vaporized everything and walked away feeling completely justified. They were hurting my kid, and I would have wiped them out.

God acted differently, but He didn't have to. He acted with restraint. He acted with passion and a love I will never understand. We are the beneficiaries of a sacrifice beyond my human reason. We have received an undeserved gift with one remaining question: will we accept it?

God loves you. It's your choice whether to love Him in return. As for me, I'm grateful for a gift I don't deserve, a gift I wouldn't have had the constitution to give.

JESUS IS MY WAY THROUGH THE DAY

ROMANS 5:1–11

I don't know about you, but I have a lot of days that aren't particularly easy to live through. I'm not talking about days that have little frustrations. I'm referring to the days where I feel worn out and overwhelmed; you know, the days where everything seems out of control and completely out of proportion. On those days, it doesn't seem to matter what I do. Nothing comes out right, and I wonder if I have anything at all positive to offer to the world. I have to confess that I really hate those days.

Now I know my problems are probably minimal compared to what others face, and I'm sure other people have jumped higher hurdles than anything I've had to confront. It's just that I wonder at times whether the Lord just wants to throw up His hands and walk away from me, completely exasperated with my lack of performance. At other times, I wonder whether God is involved with my life at all. I don't believe these are unusual feelings, yet I'm pretty reluctant to admit I run into this situation all too frequently.

Funny thing, the Bible is replete with discussions about just this situation. There are numerous instances where we are encouraged to continue, even when we don't feel up to the task. We are assured God is involved in our lives and the trials we face are all a part of His master plan for our existence. Perhaps my experience is not very unusual; nevertheless, it's still trying and sometimes depressing.

Jesus loves us. He loves me, and He loves you. This is a key concept I have had to focus on to begin finally to understand what happens when I face trials. I have learned over the years that when the trial is over, Jesus is there. What's more, He was there all along. I begin to understand the trial went on from a perspective of being a growth opportunity for me, but it was limited to what I could spiritually and emotionally handle. I may have been pressed to the limits of my capacity to endure, but not to a point beyond. Why? Because Jesus loves me. That's why!

I think one of the most important things we need to learn as Christians is the depth and completeness of Christ's love for us. It's personal, unconditional, and continuous. Christ cared so much for you and me that He allowed Himself to be beaten and tortured to death just to prove it. He's not looking to trip us up with trials; rather He is intending to make us more than we are. Unfortunately, from a purely human perspective, enduring trials is often the only way we can gain the strength to manage through this life. We live in a difficult world. The only way to overcome it is to have strength gained by knowing we have the loving support of a Father who is willing to prepare, test, and defend us.

I make it through the tough days, sometimes poorly, because I've learned God and Jesus love me. I know I can cry out to them and they will hear. Ultimately, they carry me when my strength gives out, and they forgive me for the mistakes I made as things went along. In other words, I make it through my day by learning to let Christ guide me. Even when it's stormy and hard to see, He is my way through the day.

OUT OF CONTEXT, THE BIBLE CAN'T TELL YOU MUCH

1 CHRONICLES 4:23, HABAKKUK 3:1, AND REVELATION 2:29

The Bible is the most powerful book ever written. It contains sufficient wisdom to help us order our lives, organize nations, find our Savior, and move toward eternity. The historical record it contains has proven consistently reliable. The teachings recorded within its covers are as timely and vital today as they were the day they were written. The Bible is a book authored by numerous individuals over thousands of years, yet its continuity and flow make it unique among all texts ever written.

One of the most quoted books in existence, the Bible, is familiar even to many who do not accept its teachings nor understand its worth. Sadly, it is also one of the most misunderstood and misquoted books as well. Too often people attempt to attribute ideas and quotes to the Bible that either don't exist or are patently flawed when considered against the context of the text. As the three scripture references above illustrate, it is possible to randomly extract verses from different parts of Scripture that are unrelated and together make no sense. It is also possible to extract unrelated verses and combine them in an attempt to make them say something never intended. Any way you approach it, it's easy to misquote and misapply scripture. This represents a significant danger for all of us.

It's our responsibility as believers to rightly divide the Word of Truth. We have to understand the focus and purpose of the Word of God against the backdrop from which it was written. It's dangerous to take a single verse and apply it haphazardly to any situation that comes to mind. Moreover, it's very easy to misrepresent the meaning of a specific verse or phrase by extracting it from its original context and applying it to an unrelated situation. Accordingly we must be cautious when we read the Bible or listen to someone teaching from it that we affirm the original intent of the passage at hand.

In short, we need to take time with the Word of God and to study about and learn from it. That's not to say everyone needs to be a Bible scholar, but it is important to get to a level of familiarity with the text that you notice when it's being misrepresented.

The Bible tells us in the last days, many will be misled about the truth of God's Word. We need to do all we can to prevent this from happening. In my opinion, one of the best things you can do is spend time reading and re-reading the scriptures. Make the decision to set aside a specific time each day to spend some time in the Word. This may be a little difficult if your schedule is anything like mine, but it can be done.

Another thing to consider doing is to read more than just a specific verse when you are listening to a sermon or Sunday school lesson. When you review a specific verse, back up and read the paragraphs or chapters before and after the verse in question. Pay attention to who is speaking in the text and who the audience is. When you view scripture from a broad perspective from the rest of the Bible, the individual pieces will fit together, and the lessons will be meaningful, as they were originally intended.

BEWARE THE TEACHER WHO NEVER SAYS "I DON'T KNOW"

PROVERBS 2

Go ahead. Ask the penetrating question that cuts to the core of an exquisitely complex issue. Preferably the question will have a complicated subject with no clear definitive answer. Depending on the skill level and wisdom of the teacher, the answer you receive may range from the informed and thoughtful to the speculative and incomprehensible. If the teacher is particularly intelligent, you may even get an "I don't know."

In my experience, the "I don't know" response is a particularly rare breed. It most often occurs with the more intellectually honest teachers who are the least interested in satisfying their own ego. Consider for a moment some of life's more difficult questions such as why children suffer and/or die or why tyrants are allowed to come to power if God is truly in control. Certainly there are thoughtful responses to these questions. However, few are definitive final answers; neither are they applicable in every context.

My purpose here is not to try to develop the perfectly stated unanswerable question; rather it is to note that many imponderables exist in this life for which there are no definitive responses. My concern is that when it comes to Christian teaching in particular, attempts to always have the absolutely correct answer to life's most complicated questions often come up short. Frequently, teachers of the gospel attempt to answer complex questions posed to them with overly simplistic, poorly conceived responses. Too often, the desire to appear to have the right answer overrides the honest response of "I don't know."

None of us is perfect, and none of us have absolute knowledge of every topic. It takes courage and wisdom to admit it, however. Unfortunately, for the Christian teacher attempting to expound upon a passage of scripture, situations and issues arise for which there are debatable or unknown responses. The poor teacher—or is it the risky teacher—may be tempted to provide an ill-advised response that may ultimately cause more problems and controversies. Furthermore they may actually harm the questioner either emotionally or spiritually with an erroneous or misleading response.

Suffice it to say, students must measure the answers they receive to questions addressed in any learning situation. They must review the responses against the truth of scripture and ask further questions when things don't line up properly. Teachers, on the other hand, have the responsibility to honestly respond, "I don't know" when it is, in fact, the case. Furthermore, teachers must remember to qualify their remarks to the specific context of the situation they are addressing, particularly if other situations exist where their response does not apply. Finally, if a teacher is not humble enough to say, "I don't know" when it's the truth, find another class!

FLOWERS NEED THE RAIN TO GROW; INTERESTINGLY SO DO CHRISTIANS!

JAMES 1:1–18

I wish I could gain character without the requisite tests and trials. Would that I could mature in this life without having to face up to the difficulties it throws my way. I would enjoy living a life of ease with no worries and being happy, just like the cliché says. Somehow though, I know doing so is just not real. Existence in this world is fraught with difficulties and challenges that test our ability to cope and move forward.

I often wonder why we all struggle with such a wide variety of problems. Why can't life be less complicated with fewer unanswered questions and more fulfilled dreams? It seems counterintuitive to me that things often have to be difficult before they can be easy or tedious before they can be fun. But that's often the way life is. It's a reality we all simply must face.

I've yet to meet a person who enjoys going through difficulties in life. Yet the Bible clearly teaches us to count it all joy when we face challenges and trials. I think the reason is quite simple. Learning to cope with situations and circumstances beyond our control takes us out of our comfort zone. Indeed we may quickly find ourselves in over our heads, struggling just to keep our heads above water. Rarely a fun situation, adjusting to the discomfort of a setback or tragedy makes us dig deep into the core of our being to find the courage and fortitude to press on. More than that, when we reach the end of our own strength and abilities, we learn to lean on the one who loves us most, our Savior Jesus Christ.

More than anything else in life, trials teach us that what we are is simply not enough. What we can do with our own intellect and resources often falls short of the requirements of the test, leaving us but one alternative:

to lean on the one who loves us and cares for us the most. Ultimately, we learn to have faith and not to give up when it seems there is no tomorrow.

Tomorrow always comes. We may be on the highest mountaintop or in the lowest valley, yet tomorrow always comes. In other words, we have hope in each and every new day because our Father in heaven loves us. The strange thing is that we can't learn to trust Him unless we live through situations requiring assistance beyond our human capabilities. If we are not tested, we cannot know our limitations; nor can we understand our possibilities. Counting it all joy when we face various trials means learning to become intimate with our Savior who loves us and died for us. The intimacy is based on trust, trust that is founded upon experience gained through enduring hardship and even pain.

Friendship and love are strengthened when they endure trials and tests. Without these pressures, the love remains limited and the trust shallow. Only when we learn to overcome through faith and perseverance do we gain the ability to live our lives fully and abundantly in Christ.

I DON'T NEED CHRIST BECAUSE I'M PERFECT; I NEED HIM BECAUSE I'M NOT

ROMANS 3:21-31

I wish I could tell you that I am perfect and don't have any sin in my life. I wish I could tell you that I've never fallen into temptation or harbored an evil thought. I'd like to tell you that I've never lived a day with guilt or remorse. I'd like to tell you all of these positive things, but sadly they just aren't true. I walk this earth with the sinful nature my father passed down to me, the same sinful nature I passed down to my son.

And so it goes. We all live in a generation still subject to the curse Adam and Eve received that fateful day in the garden. Now you may be critical of my admitting that I have sin in my life, or you may be critical of the fact I still have trouble with temptation. That's okay. You're entitled to your opinion. The painful truth is that we are all stuck in the same situation. All of us approach life from the same place, desperately needing Christ. Our need goes to the very core of our being. It is deep-seated and pervasive.

It's Sunday, and I went to church this morning. I sang in the choir and taught Sunday school. I'll go back tonight. I need it. I need time with the Lord, time to add strength to my spirit so I can prepare for another week in the world. I'm hopeful it will be a good week, a holy week, but I know it will have its bumps and curves. I've lived through hundreds and hundreds of weeks in my life, and through every one, I've needed the Lord. I've needed His kindness, forgiveness, and love. Through it all, He has been faithful, even when I'm not.

That, my friend, is what it's all about. Nobody in the church is holy. They may try to look and act the part, but none of them pull it off. You may attend a church where everyone dresses nicely and has that Sunday school appearance. Some will look joyful; others will appear stern. All of them will fall short; even the ones who may act holier than thou will need the forgiveness of Christ. They may not jump at the chance to admit it, but it's true. But you know what? It's okay!

In this passage in Romans, Paul spells out pretty succinctly the status of every believer. The standard is perfection, holiness, and impossible to attain. You see, when Adam and Eve fell, they broke the standard and took all of us with them. God, through Christ, is the one who satisfied the Law and shed blood for the forgiveness of our sins. Christians are not perfect. They are simply forgiven. Christians have admitted their failings and pled for the mercy of God through faith in His Son.

Christians aren't perfect, but they have embraced a perfect standard. They admittedly cannot attain the high mark of holiness. But they strive for it just the same. Why do we do this? Not so we can stroke our egos; neither so we can play one-upmanship with each other. We do it because we love God. We do it as an offering of our gratitude for His mercy and love for us. Our hope is in Him because He died for us to redeem us. That's the message the church wants to send to the world because that's the message God sent to us.

CALL ON THE LORD; HE KNOWS ALL THE ANSWERS

PROVERBS 3:1–26

I wish I knew all of the answers to the questions of life. It would be nice never to encounter a problem or situation I couldn't handle with the quintessential response. I would like never to be baffled or frustrated by any of life's complicated situations. Would that life never threw me a curveball or pitch I couldn't handle? Alas, reality is otherwise.

All of us face life every day fraught with problems and situations beyond our ability to control or understand. We encounter conflicts and trying situations that cause us to question our activities and wonder about the future direction of our lives. Each new day is a collection of opportunities and risks requiring creative thinking and innovative decisions. We have to engage the issues and apply our knowledge. Sometimes we are successful; other times we are not. But in the end, life moves on.

It's easy at times to feel overwhelmed by it all. We watch as life marches on and wonder if we're marching to the beat of a different drummer or simply can't hear the drummer in the first place. Too often, the pieces don't seem to fit, and life seems to be a chaotic mess from which there is no escape.

I believe God knows our frustrations. Indeed not only does He know them, He's planned for them as well. One of the wonderful things about being a Christian is knowing the contingencies of life have been taken care of. When we observe the events of our lives, we can do so from the perspective of knowing God is in control. The Lord tells us in His Word that He is there for us and He wants to be involved in everything we do. Accordingly we don't have to worry about whether the day's problems will remain unresolved.

Now I'm not saying we won't have issues to deal with. Indeed we will. What I'm pointing out is that the Lord is in control and watching over His own. When the difficulties and challenges of life confront us, we don't face them alone. We have someone who loves us and cares very deeply about the circumstances of our lives. We need to realize God is involved in every beat of our heart, so we just need to learn to rely on Him.

So what's the benefit of all of this? The answer is simple: we are not alone. We don't have to be in control of every situation. Instead we can simply do our best to meet the challenges coming our way and then leave the rest to our Father in heaven. When we confront a question beyond our understanding, we can turn it over to the Lord and rely on Him to pull us through.

Our lives are a partnership with the Father. We don't live in a vacuum. We live with a Father who loves us. It's our job to live for Him, with Him, and through Him. He's here for us. He's here for you.

FREEDOM IS FROM THE LORD, NOT THE GOVERNMENT

LUKE 4:14–30

When Christ began His ministry, He did so with a flourish. He wasn't bashful about who He was or what He was setting out to do. In one of His first recorded public presentations, He read from the prophet Isaiah a passage pointing both to His authority and purpose. Christ was very candid with those who heard Him, church leader and layperson alike, that He intended to bring freedom to the captives.

As a Christian, I know this freedom to be the freedom from sin and death, the redemptive freedom we can know when we receive Christ as our Savior. It's interesting to me that through Christ, God communicated the message of freedom as a top priority in Christ's ministry here. That God is focused on our freedom is evidence of the underlying purpose of our existence as human beings. God created us to glorify Him and be able to share a loving relationship with Him for all time. Importantly, for our relationship to be valid, we had to be free agents capable of accepting or rejecting Him. Without this freedom, there could be no truthful, loving relationship between us.

Freedom, therefore, is a foundational component of who we are as created beings. It was a right given to us by God that defined the basis by which we could approach life. Freedom of choice gave Adam and Eve the right to obey God or not. Freedom of choice gives us the right to believe in God, accept Christ, and love one another. Freedom gives the ability to accept the limitations of love and the law to order our lives. Freedom makes anarchy possible and sets up sin as a trap.

Many today look to the government to define our freedoms for us. In fact, throughout recorded history, we see how people either enjoyed freedom or suffered under tyranny, depending on the government in power at the time. Frequently the government chose whether or not to impose servitude or allow freedom to the people. The people often were not given a choice regarding whether or not to be free. Too frequently, oppression was the order of the day.

Freedom is not, however, a grace bestowed by a benevolent government. Rather, government exists to bring order to society by measuring the combined freedoms of the people under its charge. To achieve this end, the government must see itself as a mediator, not a mentor, an agent of fair play rather than a guide.

As Christians, we need to recognize the source of our freedom is the Lord. We do not owe it to our government or those around us. We must also recognize that with freedom comes responsibility. When we have the right to make our own choices, we will be accountable for them. Freedom exists but is not a free ride. Therefore, as you live your life, look to God for your freedom and rely upon Him for the wisdom to exercise it responsibly.

WORDS WITHOUT ACTIONS ARE LIKE EMPTY POP CANS; THEY STILL ADVERTISE, BUT THERE'S NOTHING INSIDE

JAMES 2:14–26

"Sure, I'll do that." "You can count on me!" "I'll take care of it. Don't worry about a thing." Familiar phrases, aren't they? They are casual statements too many people find easy to utter but difficult to implement. Why is it so hard to follow through on commitments? It seems so often people let their responsibilities slide and they try to get by on just the bare minimum. In the meantime, those they promised are disappointed and discouraged, not to mention overwhelmed by trying to pick up the slack.

Sadly this is a universal problem. We all have the propensity to commit to more than we can possibly do and not follow through on promises. It happens for a variety of reasons, some legitimate, others not. Essentially whenever we fail to follow through or take the initiative in the first place, we injure our own character and witness as Christians.

When James wrote his letter to the twelve tribes of Israel, he understood the problem of professing faith without following through with action. It was an old problem then; it remains a problem today. People have a difficult time matching their words with actions. They tend to profess love and commitment but really don't take their words to heart. Why is this? I think the answer is quite simple, cost.

Nothing we possess in this life comes to us for free. Ultimately there is a price being paid by somebody somewhere. The problem is that most of us don't want to be the person left holding the bag. We want someone else to pick up the bill so we can focus on our own personal agenda. That's why we often find it easy to wish someone well, but fail to help them feel well by pitching in and contributing to their need. It's simple to speak; it's more complicated to act.

The Christian faith is proactive and involved. Christ illustrated this all through His ministry. When He preached to a crowd of five thousand people who needed to be fed physically as well as spiritually, He did both. Other times when people needed healing or had other physical needs, Jesus addressed them vigorously and affirmatively. He wasn't afraid to get involved, take the time, and make a difference. Even though He was God, He took on the responsibilities of a servant. That was an example to us all. That was a sample of what our lives should be.

The old cliché says, "Actions speak louder than words;" five little words bearing mountains of truth. How we treat people tells much about who we are as a person. If we consider other people before ourselves, we will be more focused on addressing their concerns before giving attention to our own. Moreover, we will substantiate our witness in a way that is pleasing to the Lord, not to mention being visible to others.

SITUATIONS VARY; ETHICS DON'T

PROVERBS 11:1–23

Not too many years ago, how a person solved a problem was considered equally, if not more important than the results they achieved. In other words, one played by the rules to accomplish certain ends, regardless of the cost or ultimate outcome because the applicable ethics were considered immovable and paramount. However, somewhere along the way, societal priorities changed, and pragmatism and opportunism overcame integrity. Suddenly it became acceptable for the ends to justify the means. This shift in focus began to blur our vision regarding what historically had been considered appropriate versus questionable behavior. Previously we would have been very concerned with the methods used to achieve a positive result. Now we simply look to the result to determine whether methods are desirable.

Reverse engineering is a great way to figure out how something works so it can be copied or improved. Reverse engineering, however, is a poor method for designing our moral standards. The problem is, if outcomes are the only deciding factor with regard to how we live our lives, then just about anything can be justified in the name of progress. If a salesperson is compensated strictly by the volume of sales without regard to whether the sales were fraudulently obtained, the wrong message is being sent, and wrong behavior is rewarded. Alternatively, if a baseball team wins all of its games by cheating and bribing the umpires, its wins are an illusion.

Honesty and integrity are quickly becoming a lost art in our society. Too often people are rewarded for flouting the rules or sidestepping the ordinary boundaries because they happened to achieve outstanding results. The ultimate impact is to reinforce the notion that positive results indicate acceptable methods. Nothing could be further from the truth.

Certainly we should always strive to achieve superior results. The Lord admonishes us to use all of the talents we've been given to do the most with our lives we possibly can. He did not, however, give us leave to be underhanded or deceptive in how we interact with others. Rather, we are admonished to live up to standards that reflect integrity and honor. We are called to achieve great things and in the process be a blessing to others.

Life is not easy. We all deal with difficult situations for which there are no clear-cut right or wrong answers. Furthermore, even Christians tend to differ about the right and wrong way to handle various decisions. Nevertheless, we need to be continually concerned with how we approach problems in our daily lives. I believe this passage in Proverbs sheds some light on how we are to approach the concerns of our day. The key throughout this entire passage is righteousness, judgment, integrity, and fairness. In short, it is incumbent upon us to learn how to deal with other people from a position of doing what is best for all concerned parties. Being honest when problems arise and devising solutions that do not disadvantage any of the involved parties can be a complicated task. Admittedly, situations arise where someone will come up short. This is a reality of life. It is also an opportunity to share the burden of a negative outcome to reduce the impact on those involved. Regardless of what arises, be consistently honest and open. Be kind and compassionate even when it is a disadvantage to do so, and be willing to suffer loss so your neighbor won't have to. In short, show the love of God to others, just as God has shown His love to you.

SHIFTING PRIORITIES: WHEN THE ORGANIZATION BECOMES MORE IMPORTANT THAN THE MESSAGE

JOHN 10

I t's been about two thousand years since Christ walked the face of this earth, yet the church is still dealing with the same kinds of problems. Ego, position, power, and control continue to plague the dissemination of the gospel. Instead of focusing on the truth, the top priority becomes growing the organization and establishing lasting institutions. People begin to direct all of their energies on getting board positions and fostering their own personal agenda rather than communicating Christ's message to a lost world.

Human nature has always been to direct energy toward improving one's position and succeeding. Generally this is a laudable goal, worthy of our efforts and resources. The same is true for a church. Growing a positive beneficial program while reaching out to a lost world is a part of the mandate God gave to us. When the gospel is taught in candor and love, the result should be souls are saved and growth of the body. Organizations, particularly churches, will struggle during their early years as they overcome the hurdles necessary to achieve their mission.

A problem arises when the organization has achieved a measure of success as it effectively moves toward attaining its desired goals. Too often the focus shifts from communicating the message to maintaining and growing the organization. No longer are the zeal and energy of the members directed toward the mission; rather they become entrenched in managing and strengthening the structure itself. Now don't get me wrong - there is a lot of wisdom in honing the organization to make it better. The questions is: better for what?

Christ consistently confronted resistance to the gospel not from external groups, but from the church leadership of His day. These leaders claimed to have God's interests in mind and were supposed to be leading the people to the truth, but the reality was quite different. Instead of working to change lives and direct individuals to God, they were more interested in developing positions of authority and reaping the benefits of power and status.

The message for us is simple. Don't turn your eyes from the true mission of Christ; bring the gospel to the lost and show the world the love of Christ. Unfortunately the application of the mission can be quite different in the real world. None of us is perfect. We all have egos and different ideas about how to achieve the Lord's work. Nevertheless, Christ commissioned us to go into the world on His behalf to share His message with those who will listen.

In the end, it is the message that must overcome everything else. We must remember, God's love is the focal point, not the tools or organizations He provides to get the message out.

JESUS IS THE CORNERSTONE OF CHRISTMAS

LUKE 2:1–20

It's that time again. People are hanging decorations, shoppers are rushing around overcrowded malls, and kids are counting the days to Christmas break. (My wife, a teacher, is counting too, but don't tell anyone). The air is turning crisp and cold as the first storms of winter deposit fresh snow on top of unraked leaves. Thanksgiving is past, and the holiday schedule is full. We're looking forward to family get-togethers and wondering how we'll pay the bills come January. It's Christmastime, and I love it.

But times are changing. The season is no longer welcomed across the country with the same vigor of bygone years. Christmas through the years has typically been a season of emphasizing peace on earth and goodwill to men. Recently, however, it's become a season dripping with political correctness as the media and general public fall all over themselves to de-emphasize the true meaning of the season. We used to sing Christmas carols, but now we sing holiday songs. We used to re-enact the manger scene, but now we file lawsuits. We used to say "Merry Christmas" to perfect strangers, but now we apologize for not considering their sensitivities. We've lost the beauty of the season by trading it for a façade. We've cut the heart out of a purposeful message of peace first offered by God Himself.

Approximately two thousand years ago, angels appeared to shepherds on an otherwise ordinary night. They announced the birth of a child who was to change the course of history. Their message was one of love and peace, hope, and promise. They exalted the name of God and didn't apologize once for their message. They stated their case, supported the Word of God, offered salvation to a lost world, and never felt uncomfortable about what they said. They were the heavenly host following through on the mandate they received from the Father to communicate a message of love.

What's interesting is whom they chose to tell. They didn't go to the leadership of the day. They didn't go to the church. They didn't go to the influential or wealthy. They didn't accept criticism of their words, and they weren't quoted on the evening news. There were no retailers present, no marketing consultants, no lawyers, or politicians. There were no military people; nor were there government officials. There were just some shepherds and some sheep.

I think God chose to communicate His message to these because He knew how they would react. He knew they would be excited. He knew they would be happy. He knew they would believe. He knew they wouldn't equivocate; nor would they question. They wouldn't dismiss the message or worry about its impact on their status and position. Christ was coming to invade the world for good, and God wanted those who would listen to know.

You see, that is the problem we now face. We are trying to communicate the message of Christ to a world that is becoming increasingly unwilling to listen. Instead of welcoming the truth, the world rejects it out of hand. The opportunity for peace and love is traded for an excuse to shop and have a day off.

Christ is, was, and will always be the reason for the season. He is its cornerstone. We Christians must strive to keep Him there, for without Him the season will collapse and the message will fail. For without Christ, there can be neither peace on earth nor goodwill to men.

MARK WILKEN

WHERE TO FROM HERE, LORD?

ECCLESIASTES 1

U p until recently, I had not spent a lot of time reading the book of Ecclesiastes. Lately, however, it has become a greater part of my life. Ecclesiastes is one of the few books of the Bible that's better read in one sitting. In my opinion, reading just one short passage can leave one wondering what's going on, which is why I've written this.

Life is often much like Ecclesiastes. It is a collection of events, both positive and negative, coming together to make a whole. If we look at the individual pieces, we will find an odd collection of mixed emotions and events that are difficult to reconcile. Every day of our lives presents a new opportunity as we walk down the road of life into which the Lord has placed us. The problem is we never know just what we are going to encounter. We may enjoy one of the best experiences of our life or the worst thing we can imagine may happen. We may be praising the Lord for an incredible blessing or crying for help with a major disaster. It can all seem so disjointed, so enigmatic.

So what do we make of all of this? What does it mean? How do we reconcile all of the apparent conflicts and questions? Honestly I don't think there is a simple answer to the question(s). I think, perhaps, that is the point of Ecclesiastes. We don't get to know all of the answers in this life. Indeed I think it is likely many of us will come to the end of our lives here with more questions than answers. But why is that? Doesn't it seem logical we should gain greater knowledge and wisdom as we move through life? Yet even with all we experience and learn, new questions seem to come.

When we think about where the Lord is taking us, what will we decide? There is no simple answer! All of our lives are different. None of us experience life from the same perspective. Rather, we confront life based upon an odd collection of experiences and beliefs that may seem totally incongruous. Yet we do have something in common. We have a Father in heaven who loves us. Regardless of what we face, our Lord is with us. The trials, the opportunities, the tragedies, and the triumphs are all a part of the life God granted to us.

Why is life like it is? I don't know. Maybe that's the beauty of it. I don't have to know why life is the way it is. I don't have to have all of the profound answers to all of life's complex questions. All I need to know is that God knows. He is the ultimate answer. There is no other that is meaningful. That's the whole point.

Our life is a gift from God, subject to the plan of God, operating in a universe created by God for reasons known only to God. So what are we to do? That answer is known. You see, the author of Ecclesiastes said all he said to arrive at one simple conclusion. The answer is elegant in its simplicity, yet profound in its impact on our lives. Verses 13 and 14 of chapter twelve say it all, "Now all has been heard; here is the conclusion of the matter: Fear God and keep His commandments, for this is the whole duty of man. For God will bring every deed in judgment, including every hidden thing, whether it is good or evil" (KJV).

SHOULD THERE BE CHURCH POLITICS?

1 CORINTHIANS 1

Power, prestige, influence, and control, although they will never admit it, most people want them. It doesn't really matter how or where they acquire them, so long as they possess them in some aspect of their lives. Walk into any office, store, school, or church, and you will find someone in charge, a person who has risen to the top. Sometimes they're kind, other times they're cruel, but they're always present. They are the power brokers, always at the top, always defending their turf, always in control.

People like organizations. They use them for every purpose imaginable. Whether it's sports, business, games, hobbies, or religion, organizations exist to coordinate and promote the common purpose of their members. Overall the idea of coordinating the efforts of larger numbers toward a common purpose is appropriate and laudable. Some of the greatest achievements of mankind have occurred only because of the combined passions and energies of people working together. Indeed society could not function without the ability to cooperate for the common good.

There is a trade-off, however, with the organized group that can prove to be a barrier to progress. In fact, it can be particularly adverse to positive achievement and new ideas. The trade-off is the desire on the part of some, or the whole group, to maintain control over their position and limit change, positive or negative. Resistance to change serves the power brokers by maintaining their hold on control and influence.

When it comes to church organizations, the same opportunity/risk exists. Individuals or groups within the church tend to find their way into leadership positions affording them a great deal of influence and control. Obviously this can be either good or bad depending upon the motives and hearts of those ascending into the leadership roles. The concern begins where egos run afoul of the needs of the body of Christ. As was the case in Christ's day, some ascend to power to satisfy their own personal desires, even though they purport to be standing for something quite different. When the problem becomes pronounced, people are lost to the faith, the work stagnates, and the church dies.

It takes people to be the church. Furthermore, it takes effective leaders to move the church toward the needs of the community. The result of this combination necessarily involves politics to some degree, with all of its inherent benefits and risks.

It's impossible to have a church without a certain level of church politics, just as it's impossible to manage any group without a political element. It is important, even vital, for us to recognize as Christians the potential pitfalls of organizational dynamics that may run counter to the needs of the community of Christ. Moreover, we need to recognize the dynamic that pride plays in the lives of those in leadership positions. The enemy will attack the church both from without and within, and church politics tend to be one of his most effective conduits for destruction. It's our responsibility to foster a servant's heart in all of our people, particularly our leaders, to abridge the risks of running the church into the ground instead of for the glory of God.

DON'T FORGET WHERE YOU CAME FROM; IT WAS THE STARTING PLACE FOR WHERE YOU ARE GOING

GENESIS 45:1–15

Everyone likes a happy ending. We like to see the parts of a story come together in a result that resolves all of the conflicts and leaves us with the feeling all of the problems were worth it. In fact, we feel cheated somehow if a story doesn't come out that way or if some significant questions remain unresolved. For most of us, resolution of life's conflicts is one of the things we most long for.

For Joseph, the story indeed had a happy ending. In Genesis, we're introduced to Joseph, the favorite son/dreamer, despised by his brothers. Joseph lived a charmed life until the day arrived when his brothers plotted to kill him. Selling him into slavery instead, they thought they had rid themselves of their problem. For Joseph, life took the worst of turns, going from being his father's favorite to being a slave in a foreign country. I think you could call that a bad day.

As time passed, Joseph had success in his new occupation, only to fall prey to the wiles of a woman who certainly didn't have his best interests in mind. Finding himself in prison through no fault of his own, Joseph again suffered a setback most of us would find wholly exasperating. Years passed, and God blessed Joseph again by giving him the ability to interpret the king's dream, resulting in his promotion to the second-highest place in the land, not too bad for a man who at one point may have been dealt a fatal blow by siblings who hated him.

Joseph's life is full of examples for all of us about overcoming adversity. Through his experiences, Joseph became an amazing leader. Because of his consistent and unwavering faith in God regardless of his circumstances, he saved Egypt from a horrible famine that otherwise would have brought that nation to its knees. Another lesson we can learn from Joseph is his willingness to forgive and ability not to lose track of his past. Joseph knew God had taken care of him, even though he had to endure hardship to realize the blessing. Moreover, the blessing was accentuated by his recollection of the setbacks themselves. Joseph realized that God uses adversity often as a springboard to opportunity. Accordingly, when Joseph faced devastating trials, he kept his chin up and relied upon God. By remembering his past, Joseph was able to maintain a balanced perspective about the blessings he received later.

When I look back on my life, I realize Joseph's experience is an important lesson for me personally. Considering where the Lord has brought me to this point, I can easily see His blessings. They are particularly striking against the backdrop of the trials I've faced and unexpected opportunities I've enjoyed. If I didn't have the perspective of history, I would easily overlook the influence the Lord has had on my daily existence. Additionally it's easier to manage through the trials because my past experience has been ultimately positive. Now when adversity comes, I can face the problems with a spirit of joy and anticipation because I am confident the Lord will be with me and bless me.

Consider where you are in life and from where you have come. As you think about the twists and turns, can you see the hand of God working to bring about a blessing for you? God takes care of His own. As one of His children, you can count on His love and blessings. Times may be difficult now, but considering where you've come from and where you're going, you need to know the future always includes hope for blessing. Only believe!

I BASE MY LIFE ON HIM BECAUSE HE REALLY TRULY LOVES ME

PSALM 116

The world is a difficult place. It contains people and problems painful to endure. While some days are good, others are bad. You work hard, hoping somebody notices, but they only seem to do so when you're having a bad day. Then there are the people who seem to be unhappy because you are happy who then make it their business to make you miserable as well. The world is upside down, caught up in an endless struggle to get ahead, continually ranking people against each other, only to tear down the ones who briefly emerge at the top.

It is easy to wonder how you are going to measure up. By the world's standards, good is just acceptable, and great is only moderately better, but neither is ever good enough. Entertainment has become a constant barrage of ranking competitions to determine who will survive the most recent popularity contest and become an entertainer, businessperson, lover, or the most likely to do something ridiculous. People are just numbers, something to be sized up and/or cut down based on an arbitrary scale of perfection the judges themselves can't live up to. The world can be cruel, callous, and indifferent, and that's on a good day.

I don't want to come across as a pessimist; nor do I want to give the impression I have a negative outlook on life. Quite the contrary, I'm very hopeful and look forward to each new day with ever-increasing expectations. But I have to tell you why I feel this way. Long ago, I learned something that most of us come to know as a matter of course in our lives, people will let us down. Even, or perhaps especially, those who love us the most tend to hurt us the most. It's painful. Then you add in the folks who don't care for you very much, and you can find yourself getting rather depressed. Needless to say, it is not a pretty picture.

There is, however, someone who won't let you down. He's someone who knows who you are inside and out, someone who accepts your bad days and celebrates the good. Of course, it's Jesus. For a long time, I wondered about this because I tended to focus on my mistakes, worrying that He was standing just off to the side, waiting to let me have it the next time I messed up. Then I read passages like Psalm 116, and it helped me begin to see the Lord in a new light.

God doesn't want to bop us on the head. (He does so when we need it, but it's not His primary goal). God wants us to live a life of love, peace, and joy founded on a solid relationship with Him. He's not interested in ranking us by the world's standards. He already knows who we are. He created us! Simply put, God wants to help us be all He created us to be by loving and caring for us. We will face trials and tests, but they are designed to build us up, not cut us down. "Jesus loves me, this I know for the Bible tells me so," like here in Psalm 116.

HAVE YOU BEEN TO THE CROSSROADS?

1 CORINTHIANS 9:24–27

We walk through life, sometimes aimlessly, other times with purpose, often reluctantly, occasionally listlessly, but always relentlessly. We wonder what it's all about. At times we think we know; sometimes we're not sure. We're convinced we know what's certain, yet often we question and wonder, *Is life a reality or an enigma? Do we matter? Does anybody care?*

Purpose and meaning; we can spend a lifetime in their pursuit, yet in the end, we wonder. The world tells us to be a success, yet it's a prize only temporarily grasped, if ever grasped at all. The prize, indeed, the prize! What is it? At the end of the day, what have we touched, what have we moved, and why? What is profound? What is beautiful? What is true? What gives me hope, and why is it real? Is there really love? Can my heart truly hold it?

Questions, endless questions. Forever we seek but rarely do we find the answers to questions we fear to ask or are terrified to consider. We look for meaning; we desire purpose. From ourselves we can have neither; by ourselves we can achieve nothing. We build ourselves up, but others tear us down. We devote our whole life only to see it discounted and lost. We keep walking.

A new day dawns; hope stirs anew. We run toward the light, hoping for a glimpse of truth. Yet before we can grasp the dream, it's gone, vanished with the dew. Another day closes; our questions remain unanswered yet unspoken.

Life is, but what is life? What is purpose, and why is it real? Do we live to achieve, or do we live just to be? Can we grasp the prize, or are we just flailing at the air? Is there an answer to the questions, or are the questions not real? We keep walking.

It's dark today. The rains came. It's peaceful and wet. There's time to reflect. The issues are less urgent now, but still they remain. My wondering continues; my wandering doesn't stop. Where to from here, and why should I go? It's raining outside; in here it's warm. There are questions to answer despite the storm. I move forward slowly. I start walking.

Movement, forward movement, is what I desire, and it's where I should go, but what is forward? I stop and consider, and then I know.

Look back and see where I've been! How could I have gotten here? From where have I come? It's much clearer now. The story unfolds. There's goodness and beauty, hope, and delight. The darkness has lifted, and I have new sight. The questions remain, but answers abound. The pieces can fit now, and wisdom is found, for I've reached a crossroads that offers me hope. I change my direction and move a new way. I understand reason and seek a new day. I keep walking.

I'm here by design. I'm here for this day to make a difference, encourage, and love. I seek other reasons, but they all come up short. This is my life to live for the Lord.

Some questions are simple, while many confound. Yet I'm moving forward with Christ as my guide. How did I get here? To where should I go? It's God who knows. It's simply mine to behold. The beauty of the new day is held by my Lord. I don't find it inside. It starts in His Word. Today I will love Him, tomorrow as well. For He is my purpose; in Him I will dwell.

Life is not simple, but it is profound. He tells me He loves me, so my hope can abound. It's true that I love Him. He's my Savior indeed. I give my life to serve Him. He gave His life for me.

I stood at a crossroads, and what did I see? A Savior who loves me hung on a tree. He gave me His life. He gave me His love. No other could offer such profound peace as the one who loved me as He died for me. I know why I am here now. I know why I am free. He made me to serve him, to love and adore, to spend my days walking with Him by the shore.

I wait at the crossroads for others to see. The Savior is waiting for those who have need. The ones who will find Him, the ones who will see, must come to the crossroads walking just like me.

"WE WILL NOT BE MOVED" IS OFTEN THE POSITION OF PEOPLE WHO WISH TO AVOID THE TRUTH

PROVERBS 4

Standing your ground can be an admirable trait, complete with courage and honor. When you stand for causes with noble purposes, you are saying to the world that you are willing to sacrifice your life to take and retain the high ground. You proclaim to the world the justice and righteousness of your position, challenging those who would question the veracity of your claims.

What happens, however, when your position is not just? What happens when you cling to a position based on false premises or indefensible ideas? How do you justify standing for something you fear may eventually be proven false? Why hold so tightly to such an untenable precipice? Why risk falling to your doom when the ideal you support proves to be an empty promise?

Most people in the world are clinging to tenuous positions, exposing them to peril beyond their comprehension. These people are not interested in finding the truth because it would somehow jeopardize the fundamental values they embraced earlier in life. Instead of considering the risks of their position, these individuals would rather remain uninformed and unresponsive to truth and instruction than consider the alternatives.

It is difficult to know how to reach out to these people with the truth of the gospel. Their hearts are closed to the discussion before any substantive ideas can be brought to the fore. Furthermore, they tend to have a considerable level of hostility to any facts presented to them, regardless of the foundational merit contained therein.

I perceive the best approach for dealing with these individuals is persistent love and compassion. God called us to love others because He knew a consistent example of love would tend to break through the barriers over time. Obviously much prayer should also be offered on behalf of the person needing Christ. The battle we have joined is a spiritual confrontation with dimensions we cannot fully appreciate or understand. Nevertheless, our calling in Christ demands that we follow through and attempt to make a difference in their lives.

It's never easy to reach the lost, but the Holy Spirit has the ability to convict and convince far more effectively than we can. Our responsibility is to provide the information and environment where change can take place.

We're dealing with an urgent need that extends far beyond simply trying to recruit new members to our churches. We're trying to rescue those we should love and care about from the destruction and peril of hell. We have a very short time in this life to move people toward Christ; therefore we must act with great urgency and passion so more will be a part of the kingdom.

WHEN THE WHOLE WORLD IS UPSIDE DOWN, CHRIST HELPS YOU TO STAY RIGHT SIDE UP

PSALM 91

Just a few short weeks ago, only a very small group of biologists and scientists could define the term "Coronavirus-19." Now the term has become a central focus in all of our lives. Additional terms such as "sheltering in place" and "social distancing" have also become a part of our lives both out of necessity and in consideration of the well being of those around us. Now we quarantine ourselves in our own homes to minimize the risk of expanding a worldwide pandemic. Everyone on earth now lives by a new set of rules. Our concepts about our life priorities and best practices are now permanently altered. People are hiding. People are dying. People are afraid. The world is suddenly a very dangerous and scary place, or so it seems.

Each generation of people born on this planet has had to come to terms with the important questions relating to every aspect of life. Some generations have fared well in this endeavor, others not so much. As we move through time, we are learning that what we do and how we live impacts not only ourselves, but also the well being of those around us. In the 1960s, the decade of my entry into this world, nobody knew what secondhand smoke was. Now it is a vicious villain seeking the lives of anyone coming into contact with anyone who smokes. Issues like faith in God (or lack thereof) or understanding our purpose for being, our actions or inactions, and not to mention our general moral makeup all acutely impact our daily existence. This begs a follow-up on an important question: are we willing to confront seriously the difficult questions of life, or will we continue to casually brush them aside, risking the calamity that ultimately follows?

From the moment of our birth to the day we pass from this world, we learn. Whether it's the mechanically complicated ability to walk or the nuanced understanding of body language telling you whether or not someone is threatening you, we spend every waking moment of everyday learning. But what do we do when the system crashes and seemingly everything we've grown up learning goes out the window? How do we cope with calamitous events in the world, ultimately our own personal world, that turn everything inside out or simply tear it in two? What is our response to chaos replacing normal, with no obvious or realistic hope that somehow the normal we knew, whatever that was, will ever return.?

During difficult times, we typically begin looking for answers to questions we haven't had to answer before. How do we shift gears from our normal routine to a dramatically unusual and likely unsettling new way of life? How do we move forward when everything we knew as normal ceases to be normal? The Coronavirus pandemic has forced everyone everywhere on Planet Earth to reconsider life's priorities. People are becoming ill and risking death simply because they walked too close to another individual or shook their hand. There is no longer such a thing as casual contact. So we shelter in place (basically staying at home and not going out much) and start to figure out ways to connect with people without connecting with people. It's interesting how experiencing a time such as this forces you to reassess your priorities. Now that we really do have the time, we can devote our faculties to considering the things in life that are truly important.

As the days have passed over this last month—yes, most of the planet's population has been spending the vast majority of their time at home for a month now—many people have considered establishing a relationship with the Lord. Many Christian evangelical organizations have become very creative in reaching out to people on behalf of Jesus Christ, our Savior. Time alone or with a small family group brings some of the more important of life's questions to the surface, forcing us to consider the possibilities of dealing with them. The more difficult and eternally oriented questions are most often impossible to push back into the shadows. As a result, when we finally get to the point of admitting we don't have a satisfactory answer, times like these will often much more urgently compel us to seek answers where we've not looked before.

This brings me to the following conclusion: There is one God, our

Creator. We are created in His image to and for His glory. He has a Son, Jesus, who came into this world to reconcile us to God the Father. Christ died a terrible death on the cross so his shed blood could cleanse us of our sins and provide a way for us to be reunited with God our Father. Finally, in order to walk with and help us each day, the Lord has provided the Holy Spirit, who among many other things, comforts and teaches us in all things.

We were created by a God who loves and cherishes us! He is always reaching out to us, offering a close loving relationship with Him. Isn't it time that you reached back and accepted the gift that is so freely given? In my experience, there is nothing greater, nothing more beautiful. The gift is offered to you as well. You need but to reach out and accept it. A simple yes is all that is required. So what will it be?

EPILOGUE: SOME PEOPLE WANT TO READ THE FINAL CHAPTER FIRST

ACTS 1:1–11

S poiler alert! Jesus wins … but actually that's just the beginning of the story!

The greatest stories ever told are not simply about how they turn out; rather, they are about the opportunities, struggles, celebrations, calamities, and a host of other elements that unfold with the telling of the tale. In other words, it's all about the adventure! Near the beginning of Tolkien's epic tale *The Lord of the Rings*, Frodo recounts to Sam something his Uncle Bilbo used to say, "'It's a dangerous business, Frodo, going out of your door,' he used to say. 'You step into the Road, and if you don't keep your feet, there is no telling where you might be swept off to.'"

These very simple words summon us to join Frodo and Sam in what turns out to be an amazing story of great risks; incredible encounters, both friendly and dangerous; and life-changing experiences. We're not told at the beginning whether or not Frodo and Sam make it through. We anticipate that they likely do; otherwise, their story might not have been easily told or even worth the telling. On the other hand, even if we knew that they would, in fact, make it, we have to read the story to learn of all the amazing experiences they endure and the incredible people they meet along the way. The story is one of risks and opportunities, perils and strife, resolve, vindication, and strength. The tale is epic not because Frodo is a superhero; rather, it's because he isn't! And because he isn't, most of us immediately identify with his dreams, aspirations, hopes, and fears, vicariously becoming a member of the Fellowship of the Ring.

There is, however, a significant difference between Frodo and ourselves. We're real, and he most certainly is not. The difficulties, challenges, and opportunities we personally encounter are also very real and very important. When we don't turn the lights on, it stays dark. When we lose our temper, there may be negative consequences. Our lives are interconnected to the lives of others. As much as we might fancy ourselves as islands in calm seas, exactly the opposite might actually be true. We can approach life as an epic adventure, a joyful celebration, a scary tale, or something in between, but however it goes, it is our life to live however we choose, whether for Jesus or not.

We need to consider the possibilities that lie before us as human beings who are created in the image of God because therein lies the source of the opportunities open to every person on Earth. Regardless of how you may feel about it, you were not thrown into this life behind the eight ball with little or no potential for achieving great things. On the contrary, as a child of God, you have the inherent ability to achieve the incredible. However, several important hurdles stand between you and great achievements. First, you have to be more than just casually motivated. In other words, you have to want it more than anyone else. Second, you need to be willing to potentially make great sacrifices and accept great risks. Third, you must be willing to fly solo, to go where others refuse to accompany you. There are, of course, other considerations as well. The point is, great discoveries and achievements in our lives don't typically arrive in our mailboxes in brightly wrapped boxes tied up with pretty red bows. Great accomplishments require a significant personal investment on our part. The question is whether we are willing to pay the price to achieve our dreams!

Tolkien was an artist. He could paint a masterpiece in your mind as his words passed before your eyes. He was well studied and devoted an extraordinary amount of time and effort into building strong and well-designed foundations for his characters. A character in Tolkien's stories had not only a name but also a heritage and a history that almost literally brought them to life before your eyes. You see, Tolkien knew that it took more than just casually throwing words together to create a masterwork. He intuitively knew such a project required an incredible understanding resulting from years of preparation and study.

Ludwig von Beethoven summarized his perspective on what was necessary to achieve something amazing. He knew that you cannot simply be very good or merely excellent at whatever it is you do. Very good and excellent are but milestones to incredible, amazing, and unbelievable. Beethoven said, "Don't only practice your art, but force your way into its secrets, for it and knowledge can raise men to the divine." Great artists understand that there is always more to be learned, and the more you learn, the more you realize the vistas of possibilities that exist far beyond all ideas you have conceived of leading up to the current day.

So where to from here? Indeed that is the question! Regardless of where you are on this road of life that God has bestowed upon us, there are more steps to take. God created a vast universe for us to appreciate, explore, and care for. He has also acquainted us with a variety of people from whom we can learn or teach a thing or two. Some will become friends, others will not, but all have a reason for being in our lives, and it is up to us to discover why. Suffice it to say, there is more to be said, more to be shared, and more, much more to look forward to. Each day we live is a gift from God. We must realize we haven't opened them all yet, but that's the point! **There is yet more to the adventure!**

ABOUT THE AUTHOR

Convinced that life's meaning extends primarily from a real and active relationship with Jesus Christ, Mark Wilken approaches his days as potential training grounds for learning how to be a blessing to others in this life. A 1982 (BS – Accounting) and 1983 (MBA) graduate of Oral Roberts University, Mark spent the first 30 plus years of his professional career in a variety of positions with a Fortune 500 company. After being diagnosed with early onset Parkinson's Disease in January 2011, he decided to retire early and pursue other adventures.

Throughout his life, Mark has learned that giving into the lives of others is one of the most meaningful endeavors one can pursue. Experience has taught him that even during seasons when life seems only to serve up curve balls, that ultimately, the love and faithfulness of God shines through. Perspectives From the Choir Loft is intended to reflect the heart of a Christian individual navigating through the uncharted and sometimes stormy seas of everyday life.

Currently residing in the Northeast Oklahoma, Mark and his wife, Leigh, have two children, a daughter-in-law and son-in-law, and two grandchildren.